MAKING

Career Decisions

THAT COUNT

A PRACTICAL GUIDE

THIRD EDITION

Darrell Anthony Luzzo

UNIVERSITY OF NORTHERN COLORADO

Lisa Ellen Severy

UNIVERSITY OF COLORADO AT BOULDER

PEARSON

Prentice
Hall

Upper Saddle River, New Jersey
Columbus, Ohio

Library of Congress Cataloging-in-Publication Data

Luzzo, Darrell Anthony.
    Making career decisions that count : a practical guide / Darrell Anthony Luzzo, Lisa Ellen Severy.— 3rd ed.
      p. cm.
    Includes bibliographical references and index.
    ISBN-13: 978-0-13-171277-5 (pbk.)
    ISBN-10: 0-13-171277-2 (pbk.)
    1. Vocational guidance.   I. Severy, Lisa Ellen.   II. Title.
    HF5381.L783 2009
    650.14—dc21

            2007041778

Vice President and Executive Publisher: Jeffery W. Johnston
Executive Editor: Sande Johnson
Editorial Assistant: Lynda Cramer
Project Manager: Kerry J. Rubadue
Production Coordination: Thistle Hill Publishing Services, LLC
Design Coordinator: Diane C. Lorenzo
Cover Designer: Jeff Vanik
Cover Image: Jupiter Images
Operations Specialist: Susan Hannahs
Managing Editor: Pamela D. Bennett
Director of Marketing: David Gesell
Marketing Manager: Amy Judd

This book was set in Janson by Aptara, Inc. It was printed and bound by Bind-Rite Graphics. The cover was printed by Phoenix Color Corporation/Hagerstown.

Pearson Education Ltd.   Pearson Education Australia Pty. Limited
Pearson Education Singapore Pte. Ltd.   Pearson Education North Asia Ltd.
Pearson Education Canada, Ltd.   Pearson Educación de Mexico, S.A. de C.V.
Pearson Education–Japan   Pearson Education Malaysia Pte. Ltd.

10 9 8 7 6 5 4
ISBN-13: 978-0-13-171277-5
ISBN-10:   0-13-171277-2

Contents

4 what matters most?

5 what's your story?

6 making the pieces fit

7 navigating the maze

E appendix

Note: Every effort has been made to provide accurate and current Internet information in this book. However, the Internet and information on it are constantly changing, so it is inevitable that some of the Internet addresses listed in this textbook will change.

Preface

areer decision making is a lifelong process. The experiences we have during childhood and adolescence help us develop attitudes about the world of work and form the basis of some of our earliest career aspirations. As we enter adulthood, our experiences, personality, skills, and values become increasingly relevant as we narrow our interests down to the two or three careers we're most likely to pursue. That's when a clear understanding of the career decision-making process becomes so important. As just about every career counselor will attest, the most fulfilling and rewarding career decisions are made by those who understand what the process is all about.

This third edition of *Making Career Decisions That Count: A Practical Guide* is written specifically to help you learn more about the multifaceted nature of career decision making as you engage in career exploration and planning activities. Case studies of career decision makers of all ages are integrated throughout the book to illustrate important concepts and clarify the complexity of the career decision-making process. Interesting and informative chapter exercises provide you with several hands-on opportunities to put your newfound knowledge into practice. You'll learn hundreds of useful strategies to help you make career decisions that will lead to satisfaction, stability, and success.

Chapter 1, "The Developmental Process of Making Career Decisions," discusses Donald Super's theory of career development and includes detailed examples of the various stages of the career decision-making process. You'll learn firsthand that making satisfying career decisions requires an increased awareness of your career self-concept.

In **Chapter 2, "Assessing Your Personality and the Way You Naturally Do Things,"** and **Chapter 3, "Assessing Your Professional Interests and Skills,"** you'll complete several exercises designed to help you learn more about your personality, interests, and skills. Then, in **Chapter 4, "Recognizing the Importance of Your Values,"** you'll have the opportunity to learn how important it is to fully consider your work and core life values when making career decisions.

In **Chapter 5, "Exploring Your Life Themes,"** you'll be encouraged to think about your "life story," creating a narrative to describe some of the more salient themes in your life and how they relate to career decision making. You'll begin to recognize how other people in your life are essentially characters in your life story, playing important roles in the plot that underlies your story.

In **Chapter 6, "Integrating Information About Yourself,"** you'll evaluate your career-related self-concept and make some initial career decisions based on the results of assessments and exercises you'll complete in Chapters 2 through 5. As Chapter 6 concludes, you'll be encouraged to narrow your list of career options to the four or five that seem most worthy of continued exploration.

Chapter 7, "Methods of Career Exploration," presents information about multiple resources that can be used for gathering career-related information. The chapter includes descriptions of the online *Occupational Outlook Handbook*, the comprehensive O*NET system, myriad Internet resources, and over a dozen other sources of information that you'll find useful throughout the career decision-making process. The chapter also discusses helpful hints and strategies regarding informational interviewing, job shadowing, and the importance of part-time and volunteer work experiences as valuable methods of career exploration.

Chapter 8, "Identifying and Overcoming Barriers," invites you to think constructively about the role of barriers in the career decision-making process. After learning about the differences between internal and external barriers, you'll complete a series of exercises to assist you in identifying career-related barriers and developing strategies for overcoming them.

With an increased awareness of your self-concept and a clearer understanding of the career decision-making process, you'll be prepared to narrow your career options even further in **Chapter 9, "Making a Tentative Career Decision."** After emphasizing that career decisions are usually still tentative at this point in the process, the chapter introduces a useful, systematic method of setting career goals and considering educational and training opportunities. Chapter 9 also includes an expanded discussion of selecting a major to help you better understand the link between career goals and college majors. The chapter concludes by introducing the concept of Planned Happenstance, emphasizing the importance of taking advantage of seemingly random events as you continue the process of career development.

This third edition of *Making Career Decisions That Count: A Practical Guide* includes several new features. This edition provides you with the latest information about the world of work, summarizing contemporary career information resources, and updating all Internet and bibliography references. Perhaps most significant is an expanded coverage of career assessments, with entire chapters devoted to assessments of (a) personality, (b) interests and skills, (c) values, and (d) life themes. The coverage of career narratives and life themes in Chapter 5 represents the latest thinking in the field of career development, helping you recognize the importance of your story in career decision making.

At the end of each chapter, you'll find a new feature, "Key Concepts to Remember." These key concepts capture the primary learning objectives associated with each chapter. This feature, coupled with the "Questions for Critical Thought" feature at the end of each chapter, gives you an opportunity to critically evaluate the information presented throughout the book. As college and university professors and researchers have discovered over the years, the more critically you're able to think about and process new information, the more likely you are to remember and apply that information over time.

For readers who are interested in obtaining part-time, volunteer, or full-time work experience as a means of career exploration, Appendix D summarizes several job search strategies to help you identify and seek employment opportunities. Finally, as in previous editions, Appendix E includes a questionnaire to assist you in evaluating the degree to which your current (or future) employment gives you the satisfaction and enjoyment that you would ideally experience in a job.

Instructors using this text in class will want to make sure they receive a copy of the *Instructor's Manual and Resource Guide*, which accompanies *Making Career Decisions That Count: A Practical Guide*. Online PowerPoint slides to support your classroom presentations are available through the Instructor's Resource Center at www.prenhall.com.

Both seasoned veterans who have taught career-planning and exploration courses for many years and rookies who are teaching the course for the first time will appreciate the comprehensive nature of the *Instructor's Manual and Resource Guide*. Included in each chapter of the *Instructor's Manual and Resource Guide* (corresponding with chapters of the book) are chapter overviews, learning objectives, key concepts, proposed lecture outlines, suggested activities, and additional resource materials. The manual also provides instructors with sample course syllabi, presentation masters, a final exam, contact information for publishers of career resource materials, and an expanded listing of useful Internet sources and World Wide Web sites related to career planning and exploration.

Helping college students make career decisions that will provide them with satisfaction and success was first and foremost in our minds as we worked on this edition of the book. To that end, it is our sincere hope that those who read the book and invest an appropriate amount of time and energy into the process will be well on the road to making career decisions that count!

ACKNOWLEDGMENTS

We are indebted to numerous individuals whose assistance during the preparation of this book was invaluable. First and foremost, we are extremely grateful to each and every member of the Prentice Hall staff. Their dedication to the success of this project was apparent at every stage along the way. The guidance and support provided by Sande Johnson is especially noteworthy. We also appreciate the helpful comments of the reviewers of the second edition of the book who provided valuable suggestions for improvement that guided our work on the third edition: Yvette Getch, University of Georgia; Lea Beth Lewis, California State University, Fullerton; Judith J. Pula, Frostburg State University, Patricia Griffin, Fort Hays State University; and Shawn Forney, Idaho State University.

We also wish to thank the many students, professors, career counselors, and clients we have known over the years who have contributed directly or indirectly to the content of this book. We hope you'll benefit from the incorporation of these ideas into this edition.

Finally, we both wish to dedicate this book to our amazing friends and families for their endless love and genuine support of our efforts to write a book that we truly hope will make a meaningful difference in the lives of those who read it.

—Darrell Anthony Luzzo and Lisa Ellen Severy

Around We Go

THE DEVELOPMENTAL PROCESS OF MAKING CAREER DECISIONS

Online mapping programs make it easy to plug in an address and wait for turn-by-turn directions complete with colorful graphics. Wouldn't it be great if such a program were available for your life? Just plug in your coordinates, fill up the tank, put it in drive, and off you go! While such a program does not exist as yet, you can develop the tools you need to set your course and plot your destination. As with online mapping, you will also need to learn how to adjust those plans as unforeseen obstacles as well as distracting curiosities grab your attention. If you share the hope that most people do (namely that your career choice will bring you satisfaction, stability, and success), then it's important to learn how to reach your career destination.

The purpose of this chapter is to introduce you to the developmental process of making career decisions. In particular, you'll learn about the process of career and life development as conceptualized by the world-renowned Dr. Donald Super. You'll learn about the various stages of career development that we experience throughout our lives and the tasks associated with each stage. You'll also have the chance to reflect on your experiences and consider their role in shaping your career interests and values. Finally, you'll be given the opportunity to determine which stage of career development you're currently experiencing and which career exploration activities presented in this book are most relevant to your life situation.

THE PROCESS OF CAREER DEVELOPMENT

Making career decisions is anything but a static process. People you meet and experiences that happen to you as well as the way you respond to those experiences and integrate them into your life all contribute to your career development. Career decision making is a lifelong process that *everyone* experiences over and over again.

If you had met with a career counselor in the early 1900s, that counselor probably would have given you a few assessments, analyzed the results, and told you which occupations (based on your interests, skills, and values) provided the best fit for you. Odds are

People whom you meet and things that happen to you as well as the way you respond to those experiences and integrate them into your life all contribute to your career development.

that you would have followed the counselor's advice and entered a career that you probably would have remained in for the next 40 years. Luckily career counselors have changed with the times! It is extremely rare for a person to make a career decision around age 18 and stick with it for life. With rapidly shifting changes in the economy and the constant creation of new jobs and technologies, millions of people find themselves reliving the career decision-making process year after year. That's why many career counselors use the phrases "career development" or "career transitions" when referring to the process of making career decisions. Career changes and transitions involve a developmental process that will recur throughout your lifetime. That's why it's so important that you learn about the *process* involved in making effective career decisions so that you can become your own best career manager.

DONALD SUPER'S THEORY OF CAREER DEVELOPMENT

As with just about any other area of human behavior, counselors and psychologists have developed several theories in an attempt to explain what happens during the career decision-making process. One of the most universally accepted theories of career decision making was developed by Dr. Donald Super, whose theory of career and life development was one of the first to describe career decision making as a developmental process that spans one's entire lifetime. Super believed that the degree to which a given individual's career development is successful depends—at least in part—on how well that person is able to identify and implement her or his career self-concept.

According to Super, your career self-concept is directly influenced by your personality, abilities, interests, experiences, and values. Suppose, for example, that you have the natural ability to listen attentively to others while they're speaking. Suppose that you're also good at expressing concern for others and helping them find solutions to their problems. These particular attributes suggest that a career in one of the helping professions might be appropriate. However, if you have little or no interest in the helping professions, then spending hours and hours exploring such career options would probably be a waste of time. Super argued that the best career choices people can make are those that provide avenues for implementing as many parts of their self-concept as possible.

Career decision making is a lifelong process that everyone experiences over and over again.

Your career self-concept, according to Super, is a product of the interaction of your personality, interests, experiences, skills, and values and of the ways in which you integrate these characteristics into your various life roles. As you experience new situations, meet new people, and learn more about the world of work, you're likely to develop a new set of interests, unlock new possibilities of expressing your self-concept, and find new ways of integrating your values into the career choice process.

If you're like most people, it's very likely that throughout your life you'll find yourself in situations that require you to reconsider your career direction. This may be the result of economic changes or trends. Perhaps it will be related to technological advances. It may simply be "time for a change." Your interests may change. Your values may change. Even aspects of your personality may change. That's why it's so important for you to learn how to make good career decisions. That way, no matter when the need or desire for a career change arises, you'll be ready to tackle the challenge.

Super described career development as consisting of five distinct stages (summarized in adjacent box). Whether you're engaging in the career decision-making process for the first time or recycling through the process for the tenth time, you'll probably be able to determine which stage best characterizes your current situation.

Summary of Super's Stages of Career Development

STAGE	BASIC FOCUS ASSOCIATED WITH EACH STAGE
Growth	Learning about the world of work as you increase your awareness of your personality, interests, abilities, experiences, and values.
Exploration	Crystallizing, specifying, and implementing a career choice.
Establishment	Gaining work experiences and evaluating your experiences in occupations associated with your career choice.
Maintenance	Developing stability within a chosen career field as you seek ways to improve working conditions and increase skills.
Disengagement	Exploring new ways to spend your time away from your current work environment; might include a career change or retirement from full-time employment.

Growth

According to Super, the first stage of career development is the **growth** stage. During this stage people form attitudes and behaviors that are important for the development of their self-concept and learn about the general nature of the world of work. According to Super, our interactions with the social environment influence our personal expectations and goals. Experiences we have with other people and the work we are exposed to throughout our lives directly affect the development of our career-related attitudes and our beliefs about the world of work. Super believed that all children and young adolescents are in the growth stage of career development. But younger people aren't the only ones forming attitudes about careers and learning about the world of work. Many adults—especially those who are still learning about career opportunities—find themselves in the growth stage, too.

CASE STUDIES TO CONSIDER

Lauren

Lauren was a 21-year-old woman characteristic of someone in the growth stage of career development. She was in her junior year at a university, where she had been majoring in education. Lauren was the first person in her family ever to go to college. Her mother and father were extremely supportive of her desire to obtain a college degree, but—primarily because of their lack of college experience—they weren't able to offer Lauren sound advice and direction regarding the educational process.

Nevertheless, Lauren was aware that career counseling and academic advising services were available at the university, so she met with a career counselor to begin that process. One of the first things Lauren talked about was her decision to major in education. She explained to her counselor that she originally decided education would be a good avenue to pursue because there seemed to be a lot of available teaching jobs in the area. It was very clear rather quickly, however, that Lauren was not really interested in a career in education. She wanted to find a major that would be more appropriate for her.

As Lauren continued meeting with her career counselor, it became apparent that she was still forming some general attitudes about work and was learning about her self-concept. Although she had not yet begun the actual career exploration process, she was ready and willing to engage in exploratory activities. Her willingness to take the time and expend the effort to make an effective career decision proved helpful. Today Lauren is employed as a speech pathologist and finds great satisfaction in her work.

Exploration

The second stage of the career development process is **exploration**, considered by many to be the heart of the career decision-making process. Super described the exploration stage of career development as consisting of three major developmental tasks: crystallizing, specifying, and implementing a career choice.

Crystallizing

During the crystallizing task, career dreaming occurs. Some of the options identified during the crystallizing period might someday be realized, but most of the options identified at this point are more idealistic than realistic.

CASE STUDIES TO CONSIDER

Tempest

Tempest was a star basketball player and sophomore political science major at a large southern university. Her primary goal was to continue her athletics career by playing in the WNBA, but she also wanted to prepare herself for life after basketball. When she first went to counseling she had an impressive list of things she wanted to be from astronaut to zoologist! Her mother was a local politician and her father a physician, and Tempest had the confidence to know that she could do anything she set her mind to. Tempest exemplified the *crystallizing* stage in that she was dreaming and fantasizing about all kinds of possibilities. Rather than asking her to narrow down her list or "get real" in terms of her goals, the counselor encouraged her to explore and learn more about the fields that held the most curiosity for her. During this exploration period, she learned a great deal about many fields, which eventually helped her discard options in which the reality did not measure up to the idealistic notions she held. Tempest suffered a number of injuries while in college and eventually decided to give up her goal of playing in the WNBA. She took a year off after school to work in various health-care settings and eventually went on to medical school.

Effective career decision making requires an element of dreaming about a variety of career futures. One of your career dreams might be a very unrealistic option. But there usually comes a time when it's important to shift from several unrealistic career goals to a few more realistic options.

Specifying

The second major developmental task of the exploration stage of career development is **specifying**. The specifying task of career exploration involves narrowing down career aspirations to a few options worthy of more detailed exploration.

CASE STUDIES TO CONSIDER

Gabriella

Consider the case of Gabriella, a 38-year-old woman whose youngest child recently entered kindergarten. After several years of enjoying a career as a homemaker and dabbling in various types of arts and crafts, Gabriella decided to return to college.

In order to help focus her time and make the best use of her tuition money, Gabriella decided to spend a few months researching several careers that interested her.

Gabriella began the exploration process by looking into nursing, teaching, engineering, and court reporting. She also considered starting up a business of her own. It was apparent to Gabriella that many of the careers she originally considered weren't very realistic options after all. Some (e.g., teaching and engineering) required more education than she was willing to complete. Others (e.g., court reporting and nursing) didn't allow her the flexibility that she was seeking in a new career. Gabriella was a prime example of someone working through the specifying task of career exploration.

Implementing

The third and final task of the exploration stage of career development involves **implementing** a career choice. As we begin to narrow career options and work toward making a tentative career choice, we need to strive for an increased understanding of our career self-concept. Taking into account our personality, interests, abilities, experiences, and values, coupled with an informed awareness of the world of work, we're equipped with the tools needed to make high-quality career decisions. Implementing a career choice means obtaining relevant education and/or training related to an occupation. It's an advanced phase of career exploration but *not* the end of it.

For an example of someone who is experiencing the early stages of implementing a career choice, let's return to Gabriella. After narrowing down her list of career options during the specifying period of exploration, in the implementing phase

Gabriella focused on careers that would allow her to fully implement her self-concept. She tried to figure out which career options fit best with her personality, abilities, interests, experiences, and values. Careful analysis of information Gabriella gathered helped her conclude that starting up her own arts and crafts business was the best option to pursue. Gabriella attended small-business seminars, acquired skills associated with running a business, and even obtained a small-business loan from the government.

The majority of the chapters in this book focus on the exploration stage of career development. In each chapter, you'll learn how to integrate your self-concept, your knowledge about the world of work, and your understanding of employment opportunities to make the very best career decisions you possibly can.

Establishment

Once you've completed the exploration stage of career development, you'll enter the **establishment** stage, where you'll gain work experience associated with your career choice. It's a time for trying out your choice to determine if it's a good one.

CASE STUDIES TO CONSIDER

Roberto

Roberto was in the process of changing careers. After 15 years of working for the same company, Roberto decided that being a draftsperson wasn't as challenging or rewarding as it once was. After several months of career exploration, Roberto decided to pursue a career in radio broadcasting.

Roberto always had an interest in radio and even worked for a commercial radio station part-time during college. When it was time to declare a major, however, Roberto was afraid he might be discriminated against because of his Hispanic background when it came to finding a full-time job in the radio industry. He knew that the job market in radio was extremely tough to break into, and he wasn't aware of many Hispanic people who ever made it in broadcasting.

After Roberto and his career counselor talked about barriers presented by discrimination and the many avenues for overcoming these barriers (discussed later in this book), Roberto gained some of the confidence he needed to pursue his lifelong interest in radio. Soon thereafter he obtained a newscasting position at a local radio station. During the first few months on the job, Roberto gained a much better sense of what a career in radio broadcasting was all about. He learned about advancement possibilities within the industry, discovered what skills he needed to develop, and gained a clearer perspective about broadcasting careers in general.

During this initial employment phase, Roberto learned that he enjoyed broadcasting even more than he thought he would. Today Roberto is the general manager of one of the most popular radio stations in Los Angeles and has become a role model for other Hispanic broadcasters.

Maintenance

The fourth stage of the career development process is the **maintenance** stage, where stability within a particular career becomes the primary objective. Most persons in the maintenance stage continue to improve working conditions and experience growth and development within their chosen careers. Others, however, realize that they're in need of a different career altogether.

CASE STUDIES TO CONSIDER

Janelle

Janelle was a participant in a career counseling group for college alumni. She had been an elementary school teacher for 12 years and was well established in that role. While she enjoyed the stability of the *maintenance* stage of her teaching career, she was becoming bored and was frustrated with some of the political aspects of working in public education. Although she had not definitely decided to leave teaching, she wanted to explore other opportunities. Janelle participated in all of the group activities and began listing careers that were related to teaching but that held more excitement for her. She then engaged in research surrounding alternative education for at-risk students and was connected with a wilderness program for youth offenders. Over the next year, she took evening courses in counseling and eventually began working with the same program. While Janelle's teaching career moved from the *maintenance* stage to the *disengagement* stage of development, her youth programming career moved from the *implementing* stage to *establishment*.

Disengagement

In the last stage of career development, **disengagement**, there is a reduction in the role that particular work plays in one's life. Individuals in the disengagement stage make a decision to retire or to change careers altogether. Keeping in mind that career decision making is a lifelong process, it's important to note that disengagement can occur several times throughout one's work history. Eventually the disengagement stage is when people retire from work altogether, but for many people disengagement represents a transition from one career to another.

Remember, career decision making is a developmental process that varies from person to person. You may find yourself in the growth stage of development at the same time that one of your friends who's the same age you are seems to be pretty well established in a career and has moved on to the stage of maintenance. You might be disengaging from a career that you thought you'd be in until retirement. Perhaps you're now faced with the need to go back and reacquaint yourself with the world of work and begin the process of career exploration all over again. If so, don't despair. As mentioned earlier, recycling through the stages of career development is becoming more and more of a reality for almost everyone.

DETERMINING WHERE YOU ARE IN THE PROCESS

If you learn *how* to engage in effective career exploration, you'll master the tools needed for making good career decisions. Learning about the career decision-making process begins as you increase your self-understanding. Exercises 1.1, "Your Career Autobiography," and 1.2, "Identifying Your Career Needs," will assist you in determining where you are in the career decision-making process. Then in later chapters you'll complete several exercises that will assess your personality, interests, abilities, experiences, values, and life themes. Each of these exercises will increase your awareness of your self-concept as you prepare to embark on the important journey of career exploration and planning.

EXERCISE 1.1   *YOUR CAREER AUTOBIOGRAPHY*

This exercise is designed to help you figure out where you are in terms of the five developmental stages of career decision making.

In the space provided on the next page, write a brief, informal autobiography of experiences in your life that are relevant to your career development. You might begin by describing your career dreams, including occupations you named when you were young and someone asked you, "What do you want to be when you grow up?" Discuss how your career dreams have influenced some of the decisions you've made up to this point.

Also be sure to list any jobs, volunteer work, or internships you've had. Explain how these experiences provided you with information about your interests and skills. Hobbies, leisure activities, and athletic participation also should be included in your autobiography.

Be sure to mention any significant events that have played a role in previous career decisions. Reflect upon the many ways that your cultural and ethnic background, socioeconomic status, gender, and religious beliefs have influenced your career decisions.

Finally, conclude your autobiography with a discussion of the various career issues you're facing today and strategies you plan to use to address these issues.

Before you actually begin to write your autobiography, take some time to think about and brainstorm what you want to include in it. Self-reflection is especially important in this exercise.

Many students we've worked with over the years claim that there isn't much for them to include in a career autobiography at this point. They mention that they've only held a couple of part-time jobs over the years and don't have any work experience worth mentioning.

Perhaps you find yourself in the same situation. If so, remember that most of your important decisions could be considered career related. If you are in high school, what extracurricular activities do you do? If you are in college, how did you choose where to attend school? Think about part-time work experiences, things you've volunteered to help with, or things you've done with family and friends. All of these things are important in your life, so they are important in your story. The degree to which you've enjoyed any previous experiences plays an important role in career decision making. *All* of your thoughts and feelings about making career decisions—whether seemingly insignificant or not—should be included in your autobiography.

Topics to consider as you prepare your autobiography include the following:

- Career dreams
- Previous paid employment experiences
- Volunteer experiences
- Internship activities
- Hobbies
- Leisure interests
- Athletic participation
- Ethnic background and heritage
- Socioeconomic status
- Gender roles
- Current educational status
- Current employment status
- Questions about your future
- Careers that seem interesting to you
- Career-related issues you're facing

Career Autobiography

_____

_____

_____

_____

_____

_____

_____

_____

_____

_____

_____

_____

_____

_____

_____

_____

_____

_____

_____

_____

_____

_____

_____

_____

_____

_____

_____

_____

_____

_____

(If you need additional space for your story, please attach extra pages.)

EXERCISE 1.2   *IDENTIFYING YOUR CAREER NEEDS*

By completing your autobiography, you've probably learned something about yourself and about your career development up to this point. You can greatly increase your awareness of your self-concept by reflecting on experiences.

To determine which developmental stage you're in now, go back to your autobiography and highlight (or draw a circle around) any information that describes your *current situation*. Although most of this material will probably be at the end of your autobiography, there may be reference to your current career status in earlier portions of your autobiography as well. *Any* information that explains issues you're facing or the decisions you're hoping to make in the near future should be highlighted in some way to signify its relevance to your current situation.

Now compare the information you've highlighted in your career autobiography with the chart in Table 1.1. Check the boxes that correspond with the stages of career development that you most directly identify with at this time. Once you've completed this exercise, you should have a pretty good idea of where you are in the career development process.

The far right column of the table suggests the career needs you're likely to be facing at this point in your career development, along with the chapters of this book that you'll find especially helpful in your current developmental stage.

TABLE 1.1   *Summary of career development stages.*

STAGE OF CAREER DEVELOPMENT	TYPES OF TASKS	SAMPLE AUTOBIOGRAPHY STATEMENTS	CAREER NEEDS
☑ Growth	(1) Forming work attitudes and behaviors	"I'm trying to figure out what I really want to do in life."	Learn about your self-concept (Chapters 1–5)
	(2) Learning about the world of work	"I'm gathering lots of information about the job market."	Find out about trends in the labor market (Chapter 7)
			Get an idea of future projections for some careers (Chapter 7)
			Determine your relevant interests and abilities (Chapters 1–6)
			Familiarize yourself with your work values (Chapter 4)
☐ Exploration	(1) Identifying career dreams	"I've always wanted to be a . . ."	Reflect on the careers you've always dreamed about (Chapters 1–5)
	(2) Trying to narrow a list of career possibilities	"There are several occupations that interest me. I need to figure out which are realistic."	Develop a list of career options (Chapter 6)
			Narrow your list to realistic options (Chapters 6 and 7)
	(3) Determining your self-concept as it relates to the career decision-making process	"I'm not sure if I'll be really happy if I pursue *that* career."	Match your self-concept with a career choice (Chapters 6 and 7)
		"I'm wondering if it will be a career that I will enjoy for years to come."	Gather information about various careers (Chapter 7)

(continued)

STAGE OF CAREER DEVELOPMENT	TYPES OF TASKS	SAMPLE AUTOBIOGRAPHY STATEMENTS	CAREER NEEDS
	(4) Deciding which career options to research	"Now I need to figure out which careers I need more information about."	Read about job trends for specific career areas (Chapter 7)
			Gather information about options you're pursuing (Chapter 7)
			Identify potential barriers to career success (Chapter 8)
			Learn ways to overcome barriers to success (Chapter 8)
			Make a tentative career decision (Chapter 9)
			Set some clearly defined career choice goals (Chapter 9)
			Set up a timeline for realizing your goals (Chapter 9)
❏ Establishment	(1) Gaining work experiences related to your career choice	"I'm currently working in a job that will allow me the chance to see if I really want to pursue that career or not."	Continue the process of self-awareness (Chapters 1–5, 9)
	(2) Trying to determine the value of your choices	"Now that I'm working in this field, I'm not sure that my job is really meeting my needs."	Decide whether your values are being addressed in your current job (Chapter 4)
	(3) Continuing to increase self-understanding	"I'm learning a lot about myself as I continue to work in this field."	Set goals for gaining new experiences in a career area (Chapter 9)
	(4) Beginning to stabilize within a career	"I'm satisfied with my current career."	Evaluate current job satisfaction (Appendix E)
❏ Maintenance	(1) Determining whether your current career situation is providing adequate satisfaction and fulfillment	"Lately I've been trying to determine whether I'm truly happy doing what I'm doing."	Determine whether to remain in a current job (Chapters 1–5)
		"I'm starting to think that maybe I should find out about other careers."	Evaluate current job satisfaction (Appendix E)
	(2) Searching for ways to increase job mobility	"Right now I'm trying to determine whether there is any chance that I might be promoted in the future."	Learn about other careers related to your job (Chapter 7)
	(3) Learning about other career options related to your current occupation	"I'm hoping that I will find some other jobs similar to my current one that I can consider applying for."	Learn about methods for locating new job opportunities (Appendix D)
❏ Disengagement	(1) Considering a new job or career change	"I'm pretty sure that I want to find a new job. This one is getting old."	Determine the appropriateness of a career change (Chapters 6 and 7, Appendix E)

As you can see, the main focus of this book is on the process of career exploration. So, now that you're aware of how the chapters that follow apply to your particular developmental stage, let the journey begin!

QUESTIONS FOR CRITICAL THOUGHT

1. Why is career decision making considered a *developmental* process?
2. How can you learn more about your self-concept (i.e., your personality, interests, skills, experiences, and values) as it relates to making career choices?
3. What types of experiences are helpful for someone to have during the exploration stage of career development?
4. Why is it important to consider the educational and work-related experiences you've had as you begin the exploration stage of career decision making?

KEY CONCEPTS TO REMEMBER

- Career decision making is a lifelong process.
- Your career self-concept is a product of the interaction of your personality, interests, experiences, skills, and values, and the ways in which you integrate these characteristics into your various life roles.
- Learning how to engage in effective career exploration will give you the tools you'll need for making good career decisions throughout your life.

Who Are You?

As you may recall from Chapter 1, Dr. Donald Super's theory of career development emphasizes implementing as many parts of your self-concept as possible when making career decisions. In order for you to seek career choices that will provide you with the maximum opportunity to implement your self-concept, you first need to know what makes you who you are. The purpose of this chapter, and several chapters that follow, is to assist you in the process of increasing your awareness of your self-concept by examining your personality, interests, abilities, experiences, and values. Then you'll be prepared to make career decisions that will maximize your chances of success and satisfaction.

Has anyone ever sent you an email directing you to a website where you answer all kinds of questions and it spits out a description of the type of animal, tree, cartoon character, or even the South Park kid you're most like? Perhaps you've tried one of the websites that tell you that your personality is most like Luke Skywalker, Princess Leia, or Obi-wan Kenobi. As basic and unscientific as they may be, these entertaining activities are actually informal personality assessments. Such programs require you to provide information about yourself and then compare your responses to a set of pre-established criteria before reporting your results to you.

In order for you to seek career choices that will provide you with the maximum opportunity to implement your self-concept, you first need to know what makes you who you are.

From these informal tests designed for fun to carefully constructed, norm-referenced scientific instruments (often referred to as **inventories** or **assessments**), such instruments are designed to help people learn more about who they are. With an enhanced self-concept provided by the results of these types of assessments, it is easier to make satisfying and rewarding career decisions.

THE IMPORTANCE OF CAREER ASSESSMENT

CASE STUDIES TO CONSIDER

LaTonya

Several years ago, LaTonya met with a career counselor to discuss some of her career concerns. She was attending a university where she was about to complete her sophomore year, but she was having a difficult time deciding on a major. No matter how hard she tried, she wasn't able to figure out which major would be the best choice for her.

LaTonya had narrowed down her list of options to three career fields: business, education, and social work. When LaTonya's counselor asked her how she had arrived at these particular options, she said that her choices had been based on advice from friends and family members. Her mother was encouraging LaTonya to go into business because of the money-making potential. Her father wanted her to become an elementary school teacher because he was confident that she would have a great time working with children. LaTonya's friends were trying to convince her that she would be a great social worker because of her concern for others and her desire to help people.

The career counselor asked LaTonya what she was hoping to accomplish in her eventual career choice, and she had a rather difficult time explaining precisely what it was that *she*—independent from family members and friends—really wanted. LaTonya hadn't ever engaged in an analysis of her own likes, dislikes, skills, and abilities, nor had she considered how some of her experiences could help her make a better career decision.

LaTonya and her counselor worked together for several weeks with the primary purpose of increasing her awareness of her self-concept. She completed several exercises, including assessments of personality, interests, skills, experiences, and values. Then she worked on searching for careers that maximized her chances for implementing as many parts of her self-concept as possible. As it turned out, LaTonya was more interested in a career in public relations than in any of the careers her family and friends were encouraging her to consider. She decided to pursue a career in public relations, and today she is the head of a large public relations firm in New York City.

Career counselors have long recognized the importance of assessing personality, interests, skills, experiences, and values when working with clients of all ages. It's not uncommon for counselors to administer several inventories or assessments to clients who seek their assistance. The results of such inventories often provide both the client and the counselor with important information to consider in the career decision-making process.

CASE STUDIES TO CONSIDER

Gonzalo

Gonzalo was a 37-year-old electrical engineer employed as a shift supervisor at a large engineering firm in the Southwest. After 13 years at the same company, even though he had received promotions over the years, Gonzalo was no longer as satisfied with his career as he had once been.

While he still enjoyed the emphasis on math and science that a career as an electrical engineer provided, he didn't enjoy working in a supervisory role, and the work wasn't fun any more.

Gonzalo told his career counselor about a new interest he had developed: working with adolescents. Gonzalo had volunteered to serve as a Cub Scout leader in his community and had discovered that he thoroughly enjoyed working with youth. As a result, Gonzalo had also volunteered to coach a soccer team, and he looked into the possibility of increasing his involvement in other youth activities in the community. Apparently, Gonzalo had developed an interest in working with adolescents but was unable to find an easy way to integrate that new interest into his work environment.

Gonzalo completed several personality, interest, and skills inventories that helped him make the eventual decision to pursue a career teaching high school math and coaching. Gonzalo might never have considered a career in education if he hadn't been willing to invest the time and energy necessary to reevaluate his self-concept. The career assessment results verified his interests and abilities in working with adolescents.

Our interests aren't the only aspects of ourselves that change: our job-related abilities and experiences, as well as our values, also change over time. That's why periodic assessments of all aspects of our self-concept—our personality, interests, abilities, experiences, *and* values—can be so important when we're making career decisions.

Whether you're working with a career counselor, a course instructor, or on your own, you need to remember to use vocational assessments carefully. As with any tool, there are appropriate, helpful ways to use career assessments as well as ways that could cause damage. Vocational assessments are great ways to gather information, but it is important to think about that information critically and decide if the results really fit for you. For example, many vocational assessments are norm referenced, meaning your answers are compared to a group of other peoples' answers. If you really want to know how you are similar or different from that group, you have to know if that group represents people like you. If you are a female freshman in college who has never held a job and the instrument you are using includes a norm group of men who are getting ready to retire, you would need to look at your results with a more critical eye. This is not to say that norm-referenced assessments cannot be helpful; indeed, they can prompt your thinking about yourself and your needs in many ways, but think of them more as information sources than "answers" to your life questions. Many clients come to career counselors and ask for "that test that will tell me what I should be." The fact of the matter is that a test that is that powerful and all-inclusive just doesn't exist. The power of creating your career lies not with a test, but within you!

> *Many clients come to career counselors and ask for "that test that will tell me what I should be." The fact of the matter is that a test that is that powerful and all-inclusive just doesn't exist. The power of creating your career lies not within a test, but within you!*

ASSESSMENT OF PERSONALITY

One of the best ways to begin the process of gathering information about yourself is to consider your personality. Your **personality** is your way of perceiving the world and the things that happen to you. It's the way you naturally do things and generally tend to handle things. As you may already know, psychologists have discovered that our personalities are influential in the development of our attitudes and behavior.

One way to learn more about your personality is to complete a personality or temperament inventory. One of

Four Dimensions of Personality

EXTRAVERSION VERSUS INTROVERSION

(E) Extraversion: Focusing your perceptions and judgments about things based on the external world of actions, objects, and persons

(I) Introversion: Focusing your perceptions and judgments about things based on the internal world of concepts and ideas

SENSING VERSUS INTUITION

(S) Sensing: Perceiving information primarily in terms of concrete facts and details

(N) Intuition: Perceiving information primarily in terms of meanings, concepts, and relationships

THINKING VERSUS FEELING

(T) Thinking: Making judgments and decisions primarily on the basis of logic and objective analysis

(F) Feeling: Making judgments and decisions primarily on the basis of personal, social, and subjective values

JUDGMENT VERSUS PERCEPTION

(J) Judgment: Preferring order, closure, and structure when dealing with others

(P) Perception: Preferring flexibility, openness, and a free flow of information when dealing with others

the most popular measures of personality used to help students make career decisions is the Myers-Briggs Type Indicator, commonly referred to as the MBTI. If you have the chance to complete the MBTI, you'll probably want to take advantage of that opportunity. Learning more about your personality type will help you increase your awareness of your self-concept.

*Your **personality** is your way of perceiving the world and the things that happen to you.*

The MBTI is based on a theory of psychological types developed by Dr. Carl Jung. According to Jung, there are four personality dimensions that interact with one another to determine a person's psychological type. These four dimensions of personality are briefly described in the box below.

Your particular personality or psychological type is determined by combining your preferences in each of these four dimensions. For example, if you're the type of person who focuses your perception and judgments primarily on the external world of actions, objects, and persons (Extraversion), perceives information primarily in terms of meanings, concepts, and relationships (Intuition), makes judgments on the basis of personal, social, and subjective values (Feeling), and prefers flexibility, openness, and a free flow of information when dealing with the external world (Perception), then your psychological type would be characterized as Extraversion-Intuition-Feeling-Perception, or ENFP for short.

The developers of personality assessment instruments have found that certain types of work environments and careers are more attractive to persons of certain personality types. This can be valuable information for individuals exploring career options.

CASE STUDIES TO CONSIDER

Mike

Although many people see career counselors individually, others take advantage of career counseling groups. While the issues people bring to the group are diverse in nature, many are simply dissatisfied with their current jobs and beginning to think about how things could be different. Mike embodied that struggle. Mike was a successful businessperson in his mid-40s who had progressively moved up the corporate ladder. While he did not hate his job or the people with whom he worked, he had felt his motivation slipping for years and dreaded the idea of continuing on the current path. When his career group got to the workshop section that focused on personality type, Mike gained insights into why he felt so disconnected. When he began his career, he met often with clients, worked in a team setting with other colleagues his age, and was asked to find solutions to emergencies quickly. As Mike is extroverted and perceptive, these requirements suited him perfectly as he gained energy from his interactions with people and was able to remain flexible and handle new situations. As he advanced in his career, Mike's new responsibilities were more administrative with a great deal more paperwork and less time with people. His workload also demanded careful planning and organization rather than flexibility. Mike realized that his old position suited his personality and allowed him to do things in a way he naturally did them. He found his tasks easy and enjoyable and was rewarded for his successes. While still successful, his new position forced him to do things in a way that was not as comfortable, which was leading to his distress. Mike decided to look for a new position that was more congruent with his personality and took a job with a small start-up company that required working with many people and handling multiple tasks quickly.

WHAT'S MY TYPE?	EXERCISE 2.1

Step I.

For each of the following pairs of statements, check the option that describes you best. You *must* select one of the statements in each pair. There are no right or wrong answers.

SECTION ONE

____ 1. I like to be around other people.

✓ 2. I prefer working on team projects.

✓ 3. I often ask others for their opinions about decisions I have to make.

✓ I prefer spending time alone.

____ I'd rather complete a project on my own.

____ I usually make important decisions on my own.

SECTION TWO

✓ 4. I like work that involves precise objectives and clearly defined details.

✓ 5. I enjoy routine in the workplace.

____ 6. I don't rely too much on inspiration when I'm involved in a project.

____ I prefer work that is less defined and that requires very little precision.

____ I dislike doing the same tasks at work every day.

✓ Inspiration plays an important role in my work.

SECTION THREE

✓ 7. Most of the decisions I make at work are based on rational thinking and an analysis of the situation.

____ I tend to make decisions at work based on what feels right to me at the time.

_____ 8. I don't usually focus too much on others' feelings about decisions that I make at work.   ✓   I am usually very aware of others' feelings about decisions that I make at work.

_____ 9. I'm not too concerned about pleasing other people in the workplace.   ✓   I enjoy making others feel good about themselves at work.

SECTION FOUR

✓ _____ 10. I like making definite plans about my future.   _____ I prefer leaving my options open regarding future plans.

_____ 11. I like making well-defined decisions about things.   ✓   I don't like making definite decisions about things.

✓ _____ 12. I prefer rigid, clear-cut directions when working on a task.   _____ I'd rather work on a task that's less clearly defined and allows for flexibility and change.

Step II. Scoring

As you may have figured out while completing Step I of this exercise, each section represents a different personality dimension. Section One statements reflect the Extraversion versus Introversion dimension of personality. The statements on the left side represent Extraversion, whereas the statements on the right side represent Introversion. Section Two statements represent the Sensing versus Intuition dimension, with statements on the left side reflecting a Sensing orientation and statements on the right side reflecting an Intuition orientation. Section Three statements represent Thinking (statements on the left side) versus Feeling (statements on the right side), and Section Four statements reflect Judgment (left side) versus Perception (right side).

To get a rough estimate of your personality type (realizing that your true psychological type can only be reliably assessed by a lengthier assessment, such as the MBTI), determine which personality orientation in each section you tend to associate with by figuring out which types of statements you marked as describing you best. If, for example, you checked off two statements on the left side of Section One and only one statement on the right side, or all three statements on the left side, then you probably have Extraversion (E) dominance on that particular dimension.

Indicate below your preferences based on your analysis of preferences in each domain:

SECTION ONE

Extraversion (E) ___✓___   Introversion (I) _____

SECTION TWO

Sensing (S) ___✓___   Intuition (N) _____

SECTION THREE

Thinking (T) _____   Feeling (F) ___✓___

SECTION FOUR

Judgment (J) ___✓___   Perception (P) _____

Now place the letter of your preference in each dimension (in order) in the spaces below:

Your Type:	E	S	F	J
Section	1	2	3	4

Step III. Careers and Personality Type

Developers of personality assessment instruments have found that certain types of work environments and careers are more attractive to some people than they are to others, depending on personality type. Persons who identify more with Extraversion than Introversion, for example, are probably going to be much more satisfied in a career that involves a lot of opportunity to work with others in a group or team setting. On the other hand, individuals with an Introversion orientation are probably much more satisfied in careers that maximize opportunities to work alone or in one-on-one situations.

Sensing individuals usually like careers that involve concrete facts and data, whereas intuitive types probably find careers with less structure and detail much more rewarding. As you might imagine, individuals with a thinking orientation prefer careers that involve logical reasoning, whereas individuals with a feeling orientation prefer careers that involve feelings and emotions. Finally, it follows that persons who possess a judgment orientation enjoy careers with a high degree of organization, structure, and routine, whereas persons who possess a perceiving orientation prefer careers with a high degree of flexibility and spontaneity.

There are a number of books and other resources available that provide occupational titles for individual personality preferences, including *Do What You Are: Discover the Perfect Career for You Through the Secrets of Personality Type* by Tieger and Barron-Tieger. As you look through a list of occupations that match your psychological type, don't be surprised if a few of the occupations don't seem to fit your personality perfectly. Even though you share many aspects of your personality with other people who share your psychological type, you're not necessarily going to prefer *all* of the careers that are generally attractive to folks with that type. Remember that psychological preference is different than interest, so just because a career suits your type does not mean you will find it of interest. A list of occupations by personality type is also provided in Appendix A of this text to help you get started.

Choosing a career that is consistent with your psychological type means you will be asked to do things in a way you naturally do them, which tends to lead to greater job satisfaction. You may also be working with people who may share some of the same preferences. At the same time, organizations need diverse personality types in order to function in all situations, so having a personality type that is different from your colleagues may provide the opportunity for you to excel within a company. In other words, there are no "right" or "wrong" careers for each type, but some careers may be a more natural fit.

List below any of the careers that seem to be a good fit for your personality preferences.

_____

_____

_____

_____

_____

_____

In addition to helping you understand how you might like to interact with the world through work, understanding your personality can help you in deciding the easiest, most natural way for you to engage in the career development process. For example, people who have a preference for *extroversion* would probably enjoy talking to people about their careers while people with an *introverted* preference may prefer reading about various careers. In addition, *thinking* people may prefer facts and figures related to potential careers like average salaries and anticipated number of openings while *feeling* people would probably like to know about the types of people with whom they would be working. As you work through your own career planning, use your personality preferences to help you guide the process.

In addition to the specific characteristics of personality preferences, Carl Jung also focused attention on the larger description of archetypes. The basic idea is that there are common roles humans play that recur across cultures and across generations. For example, Jung described a mother archetype as someone who nurtures, comforts, and provides for the needs of others.

While most "type" theorists agree that individual differences account for a great deal of human behavior, the basic premise is that people of similar types will display similar behaviors. We use common descriptions of types of people to organize what we know about the world. For example, in high school, were you the Brain, the Jock, the Musician, the Geek, the Rebel? When people use these descriptions to talk about others, we make assumptions about how they will behave.

CASE STUDIES TO CONSIDER

Beth

Beth was a college sophomore struggling to choose a major. Beth had taken some exploratory classes and did not feel ready to choose a major, but the university required her to make a tentative choice before registering for the next semester. During their first meeting, the counselor asked Beth numerous questions about her interests and the classes she had taken. Her responses were generally short, and it was apparent that she was frustrated by the whole process. She believed that she was the only one struggling with this choice and that everyone else she met seemed so focused and passionate about their future careers. After spending some time talking about how common this issue is for students (whether people talk about it or not), how many students change their major at least once during college, and how majors and careers are often not related at all, Beth and her counselor started discussing the roles Beth tended to play in her life. In talking about high school, Beth became animated in sharing stories about her friends in both choir and her soccer team. Her counselor asked her how people tended to relate to her. She said that she got along with everyone and that by her senior year people encouraged her to take leadership roles like being team captain. That surprised her because there were other people who were much more boisterous and outgoing. Over time she realized that she had become a leader just by listening to people and being supportive. She was the person that other people came to when they had a problem and needed help and support. When asked to come up with a word or phrase that would characterize her role, Beth said "den mother," which she described as solid, confident, trusted, and wise. Beth enjoyed this role and being thought of in those terms. She agreed that finding a career that would allow her to exhibit those characteristics would be a good fit. As she had enjoyed her introductory psychology courses and saw careers in social services would fit her role, she decided to choose psychology as her tentative major.

Traditional career development tools ask many multiple-choice questions to help you to uncover your archetype. The following activity is designed to help you gain more information about your own personal type.

Use your imagination to dream about a tribal community. This could be on an island somewhere or perhaps in a different period in history. The focus of the tribe is on daily living and survival. In this tribal community, what role would you play? What would be your contribution to the overall functioning of the tribe? Write a story about the tribal community and your role within it. In what ways could this role or a similar role be played out in the world of work?

_____

_____

_____

_____

_____

_____

_____

_____

_____

_____

_____

_____

_____

_____

_____

_____

_____

_____

_____

_____

_____

_____

_____

_____

_____

(If you need additional space for your story, please attach extra pages.)

QUESTIONS FOR CRITICAL THOUGHT

1. How does your personality influence your beliefs and actions?
2. What role do you play in your group of friends? How does your personality help to determine that role?
3. Why shouldn't you base your career decisions solely on what you like to do?
4. How do experiences you had as a child and adolescent influence your career decisions as an adult?

KEY CONCEPTS TO REMEMBER

- Your personality is your way of perceiving the world and the things that happen to you.
- Norm-referenced inventories help people think about how they compare with others.
- Career counselors specialize in helping people in all aspects of the career development process.

What Do You Like and Do Well?

ASSESSING YOUR PROFESSIONAL INTERESTS AND SKILLS

3

ASSESSMENT OF INTERESTS

The most commonly administered career assessments are interest inventories. These types of assessments include popular measures such as the Self-Directed Search, the Strong Interest Inventory, and the Kuder Career Search with Person Match. Interest inventories are designed to help people think about their interests in a variety of recreational activities, academic areas, and work environments. An individual's particular interests are then compared to the interests of other persons who have completed the inventory and who are satisfied with their career choice.

Say, for example, that a first-year college student named Stacia completes the online version of the Kuder Career Search (KCS) with Person Match by logging on to www.kuder.com. After she completes the inventory, it is immediately scored online. During the scoring process, Stacia's responses to the various items on the inventory are compared to the answers provided by persons representing hundreds of occupations who completed the same inventory. This comparison group is composed of workers who report a very high level of satisfaction with their careers.

If Stacia's responses to the KCS with Person Match are similar to the responses provided by an accountant, then the inventory's online interpretive report for Stacia will suggest that she consider exploring careers in accounting. If, on the other hand, Stacia's responses differ greatly from the responses provided by an accountant, then the report would *not* suggest accounting as a possible career field of interest.

There are many ways to organize interests into categories that can help to guide people toward specific work environments. One of the best-known systems for classifying interest preferences was developed by Dr. John L. Holland, whose system includes six primary interest groups: *Realistic* activities involve working with your hands or in outdoor settings; *Investigative* jobs entail searching for solutions to complex scientific problems; *Artistic* activities encourage creativity and personal expression through writing, music, and art; *Social* interests provide you with the opportunity to teach and help other people; *Enterprising* interests include tasks in which you manage or persuade others; and *Conventional* interests are characterized by organization and planning. Holland's classification system is used by career counselors throughout the world to help people make career decisions. By ranking your top three interest groups and using the first letter of their names, you create a three-letter Holland code. Using the *Dictionary of Holland Occupational Codes* (available in most college/university and public libraries), you can explore which career environments share the same combination of interests. Exercise 3.1 is a short activity to help you begin thinking about your Holland Code.

EXERCISE 3.1   *HOME INTERESTS*

Pretend you're about to begin college. You're moving to a residence hall in a month and have to rank your choices in terms of where you want to live. The following descriptions were provided by the housing office to help you choose. Read the following descriptions and rank order your top three choices:

- The first residence hall is filled with people who like working with their hands. When things go wrong mechanically, the residents are more likely to fix it themselves than to call someone. A high percentage of student athletes live in this dorm. Many of the cars parked in the lot nearby are in various states of repair. The dorm is well kept and some of the residents have gardening projects going on in the quad. There are also a number of environmentalists who live here. (R = REALISTIC)

- The next residence hall is filled with people who enjoy solving scientific problems. There are a number of research labs in the basement that are full any time of the day. Although this tends to be a fairly quiet dorm, you can often find small groups of residents in deep discussions related to analyzing, researching, or solving problems. (I = INVESTIGATIVE)

- The next residence hall is elaborately decorated and you can usually hear various types of music when you walk by. Residents do not seem to keep to a regular schedule and it is not unusual to find a group of musicians in the lounge or a writing group discussing their favorite author. These students tend to prefer courses that explore ideas and creative thinking. They are innovative and prefer thinking outside of the box. (A = ARTISTIC)

- The next residence hall has a reputation for being the party dorm. In addition, the students often work together on community service projects and social causes. Rather than leading events, they are the first to volunteer to help out. The residents tend to be friendly and have a sincere desire to help other people. Most residents know the other people on their floor and consider them all friends. (S = SOCIAL)

- The next residence hall houses many of the students who participate in student government. They are natural-born leaders and tend to want to be in control of situations. In addition, there are many residents who work in addition to going to school and some who even have their own businesses already. The debate team all lives in this dorm and you will often find people in the lounges having animated discussions about current events. (E = ENTERPRISING)

- The final residence hall is very organized and structured. There are signs posted by the elevator and in the kitchen reminding people about the rules. Residents tend to work by themselves on projects that can be completed by certain deadlines. They are all extremely reliable and follow through well on instructions from others. They enjoy classes that are detail oriented. (C = CONVENTIONAL)

Now, which residence hall best reflects your interest patterns? Which one would you be most drawn to? Where do you think you would best fit in?

First Choice: _____ Letter Code (R, I, A, S, E, or C): _____

Second Choice: _____ Letter Code: _____

Third Choice: _____ Letter Code: _____

Using your three letter codes in order, what is your Holland Code?

_____

(in order from first choice to third choice; e.g., SIA)

As you will discover later in the career exploration and decision-making process, your Holland Code will come in handy as you begin to explore careers worthy of your pursuit.

CASE STUDIES TO CONSIDER

Jenny

Jenny had been out of law school for three years and was working for a large law firm in a relatively big city. As challenging as it had been, Jenny enjoyed law school very much and had also enjoyed her first couple of years in practice. While her coworkers and fellow graduates were excited to be moving into more courtroom based activities, Jenny was reluctant to give up her focus on research and writing.

In one of the sessions of her career counseling group, they went through a Holland Interest Code activity and Jenny selected *Artistic* as her first choice. She then selected *Conventional*, followed by *Investigative*. She explained that she enjoyed writing and being creative. She also liked developing systematic approaches to tasks and solving problems through research. Another group member commented that he would have expected attorneys to be more interested in the *Enterprising* category of leading and persuading other people. Jenny reflected on that information and realized that could be what separated her from many of her colleagues. The results of the activity reinforced her interests and gave her the confidence to follow her preferences. Jenny decided to stay within the legal field but to pursue a position that would allow her to do more writing, research, and organizing.

As you might imagine, results from interest inventories can provide you with helpful information in making some initial career decisions. By learning which career areas are compatible with your interests, you can explore specific opportunities that exist within those particular areas.

In our culture, careers and work are the ways in which we participate and interact with the world. In fact, a great deal of our personal identity is measured by what we do. How many times has someone you've just met asked, "What is your major?" or "What is it that you do?" In that context, choosing a major or career path is the beginning of creating your identity. Like a great novelist, you have the power and responsibility to shape your personal story. Together,

Like a great novelist, you have the power and responsibility to shape your personal story.

interest and personality preferences give you a good start in understanding the main character of your story: You!

EXERCISE 3.2   *CAREER DREAMING*

As you may recall from Chapter 1, Dr. Super used the term *crystallizing* to refer to some of the career decisions we often make when we're at the beginning of the career exploration process. Perhaps you're one of the many people who dreamed about being a doctor when you were young. If so, then what you were basically doing was fantasizing about a career that you found interesting at the time. Even at a very young age, most people have at least some idea of what they like and dislike, even though many of us eventually select careers that are very different from our early career fantasies.

This exercise gives you the chance to fantasize again, to consider those careers that you would pursue if there were no barriers whatsoever to prevent you from doing so. It's time to dream again! Forget for a moment about all of the reasons you shouldn't pursue a career you've found appealing. Instead, allow yourself to dream about the careers you'd go for if there were *no reasons at all* to stop you from doing so. List your career dreams in the spaces below:

CAREER DREAMS

1. _____
2. _____
3. _____
4. _____
5. _____
6. _____
7. _____
8. _____
9. _____
10. _____

You'll return to this exercise later in the book as you begin to integrate the results of several career assessments. In the meantime, if you think of any other career dreams in the next few days, be sure to add them to this list.

EXERCISE 3.3   *ACTIVITIES RATINGS*

To complete this exercise, simply rate your interest in each of the following activities. Use the scale shown below to rate your interest:

1	2	3	4	5
not interested at all	not very interested	neutral	somewhat interested	very interested

RATING	ACTIVITY	RATING	ACTIVITY
_____	1. Visiting a science museum	_____	3. Developing an annual schedule of important events
_____	2. Attending a seminar on public relations		

RATING	ACTIVITY	RATING	ACTIVITY
_____	4. Discussing a philosophical concept or idea	_____	23. Playing a musical instrument
_____	5. Enforcing a safety rule or procedure	_____	24. Marketing a new service to the public
_____	6. Camping in the mountains	_____	25. Diagnosing someone's illness
_____	7. Conducting a science experiment	_____	26. Working with disadvantaged youth
_____	8. Training adults in first-aid techniques	_____	27. Rebuilding an engine
_____	9. Writing a short story	_____	28. Painting a picture of a landscape
_____	10. Participating in an outdoor activity	_____	29. Talking to a group of people about legal matters
_____	11. Reviewing financial records	_____	30. Working on a farm
_____	12. Selling a new product	_____	31. Participating in an athletic event
_____	13. Learning about local history	_____	32. Working for a social service agency
_____	14. Filing important documents	_____	33. Selling real estate
_____	15. Repairing a broken appliance	_____	34. Auditioning for a musical or play
_____	16. Planting seeds in a garden	_____	35. Repairing a broken radio
_____	17. Reading about recent scientific discoveries	_____	36. Reading the *Wall Street Journal*
_____	18. Organizing information gathered from "surfing" the Internet	_____	37. Watching a Supreme Court hearing
_____	19. Teaching a subject you enjoy to a group of people	_____	38. Going to the zoo
_____	20. Solving complex mathematical problems	_____	39. Taking a psychology or human relations course
_____	21. Operating large machinery	_____	40. Fixing a broken computer
_____	22. Recording important details from a conversation		

As with the other exercises in this chapter, we'll be scoring and integrating the results of this exercise later in the book.

ASSESSMENTS OF ABILITIES AND EXPERIENCES

In addition to personality and interest inventories, skills and experience assessments also are useful career decision-making tools. These types of inventories are designed to evaluate an individual's abilities in several work-related domains. Some of these assessments are self-ratings of skill and involve nothing more than rating how good you *think* you are at certain work-related tasks. Other assessments, such as the Armed Services Vocational Aptitude Battery (ASVAB) and the Differential Aptitude Test (DAT), involve a detailed analysis of demonstrated work-related skills and abilities.

Career counselors will sometimes suggest that students complete a battery of ability tests to gather information about relevant work-related skills. The resulting information can help you figure out the practicality of various career options, thereby suggesting specific careers that you may not have otherwise considered.

Career counselors are professional counselors who specialize in helping people in all aspects of the career decision-making process.

CASE STUDIES TO CONSIDER

Shelley

Consider the case of Shelley, a sophomore attending a large university in Southern California. Shelley took college very seriously. Her family was unable to help her financially, so she had to work 30 hours a week while going to college. She wanted to be very organized in her career planning, so she wasted no time beginning the process of career exploration.

Shelley was fairly sure that she wanted to pursue a career in either medicine or law, but she was having a difficult time deciding. She met with a university career counselor for some guidance about where to start the process of making a choice. When the counselor asked Shelley how she had developed an interest in medicine and law, she described the series of personality and interest inventories (which included the MBTI, Self Directed Search, and the Strong Interest Inventory) that she had completed during her first year in college. The results of the inventories consistently revealed that careers in medicine and law were directly related to her hobbies and interests. Shelley was especially attracted to professions that would provide her the opportunity to help others, and she was confident after interviewing various doctors and lawyers that either profession would be rewarding.

Until she began working with a career counselor, however, Shelley didn't have a really clear sense of her specific skills associated with law and medicine. Most of the classes she had completed during her first year were general education courses. Although she enjoyed most of her first-year classes, they didn't provide her with the chance to explore her abilities in areas directly related to medicine and law. She agreed that completion of an aptitude assessment would be helpful.

Shelly agreed to take the DAT, an aptitude battery designed to measure a person's ability to learn or to succeed in certain work-related areas. Results of the DAT indicated that Shelley possessed many of the skills associated with a career in medicine. She scored exceptionally high on the Numerical Reasoning and Abstract Reasoning scales, providing evidence of her math and science ability and her ability to solve complex problems.

Although Shelley possessed many of the skills related to a career in law, as revealed by her moderately high scores on the Verbal Reasoning and Language Use scales, she demonstrated somewhat lower skills in many of these areas relative to her performance in the domains related to a career in medicine. Discussions with her career counselor also revealed that Shelley was less confident in her ability to engage in oral arguments and debate than in her ability to diagnose problems and work on investigative tasks. The information about Shelley's skills and abilities gathered from the assessments, along with the many meetings she had with her counselor, helped her make the eventual decision to enroll in the college's pre-med program. Today Shelley is an internist working in the Midwest.

As you engage in the process of making career decisions, it will be helpful for you to assess your strengths and weaknesses and learn to integrate that information into your career choice. As with assessments of personality and interests, if you have access to a reliable and valid assessment of skills and abilities, you should consider completing such an assessment. Exercise 3.4, "Linking the Past to the Present," and Exercise 3.5, "How Well Do You Do What You Do?," will help you begin to think about the ways that experiences have helped you acquire various work-related skills.

To complete this exercise, simply evaluate how much experience you've had with each of the activities listed below. There may be some activities that you've not yet experienced, but you probably have at least some experience with most. Use the scale below when rating your experience with each of the following activities.

1	2	3	4	5
no experience at all	*very little experience*	*moderate experience*	*very much experience*	*lots and lots of experience*

RATING	ACTIVITY	RATING	ACTIVITY
_____	1. Creating artwork	_____	22. Collecting scientific data
_____	2. Serving other people	_____	23. Selling insurance
_____	3. Promoting new products or services	_____	24. Organizing information into a word-processing document
_____	4. Hiking in the mountains		
_____	5. Solving mathematical problems	_____	25. Helping people work through their personal problems
_____	6. Working with tools to fix things	_____	26. Rebuilding an engine or appliance
_____	7. Managing other people's work	_____	27. Pondering the meaning of life
_____	8. Teaching children how to read	_____	28. Convincing people to purchase a particular brand or product
_____	9. Playing musical instruments		
_____	10. Participating in volunteer work	_____	29. Filing important documents
_____	11. Conducting research studies	_____	30. Working outdoors
_____	12. Planting vegetables in a garden	_____	31. Writing a news story
_____	13. Selling things to customers	_____	32. Finding answers to medical questions
_____	14. Drawing or sketching pictures	_____	33. Decorating rooms in a house
_____	15. Hunting and/or fishing	_____	34. Building things from scratch
_____	16. Debating a political topic	_____	35. Doing your taxes
_____	17. Finding answers to legal questions	_____	36. Helping someone figure out which career to pursue
_____	18. Reading science books		
_____	19. Entertaining people	_____	37. Selling cars
_____	20. Discussing business principles and concepts	_____	38. Designing a new home
		_____	39. Harvesting crops
_____	21. Repairing broken machines or equipment	_____	40. Reading about your local town's history

To complete this exercise, indicate your skill level for each of the activities listed below. Use the following scale for rating your skills:

1	2	3	4	5
no skill at all	*very little skill*	*moderate skill*	*high skill*	*very high skill*

RATING	ACTIVITY	RATING	ACTIVITY
_____	1. Tutoring others in a subject you're good at	_____	2. Working with animals/livestock
		_____	3. Understanding a complex legal argument

RATING	ACTIVITY	RATING	ACTIVITY
_____	4. Managing people to accomplish a particular task	_____ 24.	Maintaining a garden of fruits and vegetables
_____	5. Promoting a new product	_____ 25.	Selling automobile and/or life insurance
_____	6. Creating a work of art	_____ 26.	Working for a construction company building homes
_____	7. Understanding the meaning of philosophical ideas or concepts	_____ 27.	Researching the causes of a medical illness or disease
_____	8. Operating farm machinery	_____ 28.	Proofreading an essay
_____	9. Using a word-processing program	_____ 29.	Developing an organized method of running an office
_____	10. Fixing broken machines	_____ 30.	Handling emergency situations
_____	11. Designing the interior of a house	_____ 31.	Landscaping the front yard of a new home
_____	12. Solving mathematical problems	_____ 32.	Understanding a scientific explanation of something
_____	13. Developing new friendships	_____ 33.	Reassembling an appliance after fixing it
_____	14. Playing musical instruments	_____ 34.	Engaging in competitive athletic events
_____	15. Persuading someone to buy a particular brand or product	_____ 35.	Working as a retail salesperson
_____	16. Influencing people to agree with your ideas	_____ 36.	Researching a scientific topic on the Internet
_____	17. Understanding others' feelings	_____ 37.	Building kitchen cabinets for a new house
_____	18. Describing how a machine works	_____ 38.	Owning and/or operating a farm
_____	19. Teaching people to complete a difficult task	_____ 39.	Developing a marketing plan to sell a new product
_____	20. Managing a database of information	_____ 40.	Performing in front of a large audience
_____	21. Finding solutions to scientific problems		
_____	22. Presenting a public presentation on a current event topic		
_____	23. Showing compassion to others		

When we get to Chapter 6, we'll score and interpret the results of these and the other exercises in the chapter. But first you'll need to explore your values and gain a better understanding of how your values influence your career decisions. This is the focus of Chapter 4.

OTHER TYPES OF CAREER ASSESSMENT

In addition to personality and interest inventories and measures of experiences and skills, test developers have created many other assessments to help us make well-informed career decisions. You may want to meet with a career counselor to find out what career assessments are available to you.

Career counselors are professional counselors who specialize in helping people in all aspects of the career decision-making process. Most career counselors have master's or doctoral degrees in counseling and have completed several years of professional training. You might find it very helpful to seek the assistance of a career counselor and participate in a thorough evaluation of your personality, interests, skills, values, and life themes. You can enlist help through one-on-one counseling or in career classes or workshops. If you do decide to seek professional career counseling services, it is important to shop around and find the right career professional. Ask about specific services, fees, time expectations, and their credentials. Meet with a couple of counselors before you select one, to make sure you get the right fit. Finding a career professional is easy—you can just open the phone book and find hundreds of options! To narrow down that list, here are some things to consider:

- Most colleges and universities offer some type of career assistance. If you are a college or university student, track down your career services office. If you are an alumnus, contact your alma mater to see if services are available to you.
- Many communities offer Workforce Centers to help you in your career transitions. Not only can these offices provide you with direct services, but they may also be able to help you financially if you decide to engage in more training or education.
- Counselors are credentialed in many ways. You can find a list of master career counselors (MCCs) at the National Career Development Association Web site, www.ncda.org. A list of nationally certified counselors (NCCs) may be accessed at www.nbcc.org. Similarly, a list of licensed professional counselors in your state can probably be found somewhere on your state's official Web site.
- Many nonprofits, such as churches and community centers, offer career counseling services on a sliding pay scale that varies depending on how much you can afford. For example, some YWCAs offer complete career centers that are open to the public on a sliding scale.

QUESTIONS FOR CRITICAL THOUGHT

1. When you have the choice to do anything you want, what activities do you choose?
2. Why is it important for you to identify your career dreams?
3. Why shouldn't you base your career decisions solely on what you like to do?
4. How do experiences you had as a child and adolescent influence your career decisions as an adult?

KEY CONCEPTS TO REMEMBER

- Your interests are a reflection of things you enjoy and tasks you enjoy performing.
- Interest inventories help people think about interests in recreational activities, academic areas, and work environments.
- By finding a work environment that suits your interests, you will be asked to complete tasks you enjoy doing in a way that comes naturally to you.

What Matters Most?

RECOGNIZING THE IMPORTANCE OF YOUR VALUES

Just as assessments of our personality, interests, experiences, and abilities are important in the process of making career decisions, equally important are assessments of our values. Making a career decision based only on what we like and what we're good at can still lead to job dissatisfaction and unhappiness. Why? Because knowing about our personal values and understanding how those values influence our happiness and satisfaction are critical to making good career decisions. If your values align with your job, career, and other employees of the organization with whom you work, you'll be much happier than if your values do not align accordingly.

As you begin to consider various career possibilities, you'll be sure to benefit from a thorough evaluation of your values. The purpose of this chapter is to introduce you to the role that values play in career decision-making and to provide you with the opportunity to consider how your own personal values can be integrated into the career decision-making process.

THE ROLE OF WORK-RELATED VALUES

Over the past several years there have been many political discussions about values, including everything from the importance of family values to the ethics and values of corporate leaders to the various ways that morality is depicted in the media. When we talk about values, it's helpful to recognize the many ways values can be defined. Some of us think of values as morals or ethics. Others consider values to be important beliefs and opinions that are such an important part of who you are that you'd be willing to die for them! This may sound extreme, but such a definition helps us realize why it's so important to consider values in career exploration and planning.

CASE STUDIES TO CONSIDER

Hai

Hai made the decision to return to school after several years of working in a job he described as a "dead end." Long hours and lots of overtime week after week had taken their toll. Hai wanted to find a career that would allow him more time to spend with his two children. Even though the financial security provided by his job was comforting, Hai felt like he had been neglecting his family.

Knowing about our personal values and understanding how those values influence our happiness and satisfaction are critical to making good career decisions.

Hai decided to enroll in night classes offered at the community college. He wasn't sure of a particular career direction to follow, but he knew that he wanted a change. He recognized that by going back to school he'd be able to explore new careers and complete the necessary steps to make a career change possible.

Hai met with a career counselor to get some assistance with the beginning stages of the career exploration process. Results of his personality, interest, and ability tests validated his thinking that a career in either a math- or science-related field would be appropriate. Hai had always enjoyed math and science classes in high school, and, although he hadn't ever attended college, he had always maintained his interest in science and math. He mentioned, for example, that he was an avid member of several computer clubs. He also had developed a special interest in the Internet. He recalled that classes requiring some type of computer work were his favorites.

Work-related values, those things about our work environment that matter a great deal to us, are integrally connected with our on-the-job performance as well as our career-related satisfaction and success.

When Hai began to explore his work-related values and how they had affected his career choices, Hai's counselor explained that values are "the cement that binds our career interests and skills together."

For two weeks, Hai engaged in a thorough evaluation of his values and began to realize that he valued job environments that maximized the opportunity for self-directed work activities. He also recognized that a job that allowed for creative expression corresponded with his work-related values.

After additional exploration, Hai decided to major in computer science. He began exploring career opportunities in private consulting as well as contract work in computer programming. Such options seemed to afford him the independence and freedom that he valued so highly.

Today, Hai owns his own computer science consulting firm in Northern California and enjoys the many opportunities for self-directed work and creative expression that his career affords.

Work-related values, those things about our work environment that matter a great deal to us, are integrally connected with our on-the-job performance as well as our career-related satisfaction and success. Now is the time for you to begin to identify the work-related values you possess. Exercise 4.1, "What Makes Work Fun For You?," will help you with this process.

| *WHAT MAKES WORK FUN FOR YOU?* | **EXERCISE 4.1** |

A. Think about jobs you've had that you especially liked. What aspects of those jobs did you enjoy the most? Below is a list of work-related values associated with different types of careers. As you read through the list, decide which factors have contributed to your job satisfaction in the past or that you think will contribute to job satisfaction in the future. Remember to complete this exercise based on what work-related values *you* possess, not what values you think you *should* possess or what others (e.g., parents, teachers, friends) tell you that you should value.

Place a check mark next to the work-related factors listed below on which you place a high value.

_____ Salary
_____ Work location (indoors vs. outdoors)
_____ Benefits (e.g., health insurance, retirement plan)
_____ Stable employment
_____ Challenging work responsibilities
_____ Opportunities for advancement/promotion
_____ Opportunities to receive recognition for what you do
_____ Opportunities to develop new skills
_____ Opportunities for variety in your work
_____ Opportunities to travel
_____ Opportunities to work with tools and machines
_____ Opportunities to comfort other people
_____ Opportunities to educate or advise others
_____ Opportunities to be creative
_____ Opportunities to work independently
_____ Opportunities to encourage and motivate others
_____ Opportunities to engage in risk-taking, adventurous behavior
_____ Opportunities to supervise the work of others
_____ Opportunities to be systematic and organized in your work
_____ Opportunities to assist others less fortunate than you
_____ Opportunities to participate in innovative projects
_____ Opportunities to hold a position of high visibility
_____ Opportunities to work with other people
_____ Opportunities to influence or persuade others
_____ Opportunities to entertain others

B. The above list is far from comprehensive. List below any other aspects of the work environment that you highly value.

_____

_____

_____

_____

_____

_____

_____

C. Now rank the work-related values that you identified in Part A and the additional values listed in Part B *in the order of their importance to you.* Write in the value that is the most important to you on the first line below. On the second line, write in the item that is the second most important work-related value to you, and so on. Continue this process until you've listed all of those qualities that you checked off in Part A and included in Part B. The least important values will be toward the end of your list.

Most Important   _____

_____

_____

_____

_____

_____

_____

_____

_____

_____

_____

_____

Least Important   _____

We'll return to this list of work-related values later on in the career decision-making process.

CORE LIFE VALUES

When we talk about work-related values, we refer to aspects of the work environment that we experience on the job. Flexibility in work hours, the opportunity to interact with others, or out-of-town travel are all examples of the types of work-related characteristics that we need to examine when making career decisions.

As you continue with the career decision-making process, however, you'll also need to consider other values you possess and how they influence your career satisfaction and success. These more personal values are often referred to as **core life values.** Core life values differ from work-related values in that they are all encompassing. They represent the things in life that matter to you the most, the principles and beliefs that make you who you are.

CASE STUDIES TO CONSIDER

Dylan

Dylan worked with a career counselor through a placement company hired to help the spouses of relocating employees find jobs in their new areas. Dylan had been working as an accountant since graduating from college and generally enjoyed the day-to-day tasks of his employment. In the initial session his counselor asked if he intended to look for a similar position in the new location or if he wanted to look for something different. While he indicated interest in his tasks and a general affection for his job, he did not seem very enthusiastic. He said that he felt like his job was not very important and did not have much of a positive impact on the world. As a new father, he had become more and more aware of his desire to make a difference in the world and didn't see how his current position helped him to do that. While his job suited his personality, skills, experience, preferences, and his work-related values, it did not seem to align with his core value of community contribution. He decided to look for ways that he could apply his skills in a new setting. Eventually he became an accountant for a private foundation that raised funds for community service projects across the country. In this way he was able to continue in an occupation he enjoyed while contributing to his community.

Personality, interests, abilities, and experiences are certainly important to consider in their own right, but gaining increased awareness of values and understanding their role in career development cannot be overlooked if you want to make career decisions that count. Exercise 4.2, "Getting at the Core: What Matters Most?," will help you identify some of your core life values.

GETTING AT THE CORE: WHAT MATTERS MOST?	EXERCISE 4.2

In Exercise 4.1, we focused on work-related values, those values that are important to you in an actual career. Now we turn our attention to your core life values, those values that characterize what matters to you most in life.

Step 1. Begin by generating a list of the core values that you most strongly believe in. Allow yourself some time to think about the values that are most important to you. Be sure to consider the ways that your cultural and ethnic background, gender, age, and social class have influenced your value system.

Don't expect to be able to complete this exercise in a minute or two. The more thought you give to this exercise, the more successful you'll be at integrating your values into the career decision-making process. Remember, your core life values may not seem related to career decision-making at all. But you'll begin to see their relevance as you continue the exploration process.

Core life values represent the things in life that matter to you the most, the principles and beliefs that make you who you are.

To help you get started, the following core life values are provided to you as a reference. Circle the values that you consider most important. In the spaces provided, list any additional core life values that you possess.

✓	Achievement	✓	Health
	Adventure		Honesty
✓	Availability to my children		Independence
✓	Availability to my spouse or significant other		Integrity
		✓	Intellectual stimulation
	Church participation		Leisure time
	Community outreach	✓	Loyalty
	Education		Material wealth
	Environment		Patriotism
	Ethics		Personal appearance
	Fame		Physical fitness
✓	Family relationships		Power
	Financial comfort		Recognition
	Freedom		Religion
	Friendships	✓	Respect
	Generosity	✓	Safety

_____ Security   _____ Spiritual development

_____ Sense of accomplishment   _____ Time to myself

_____ Social status

ADDITIONAL CORE VALUES YOU POSSESS THAT ARE NOT LISTED ABOVE

_____   _____

_____   _____

_____   _____

_____   _____

Step 2. Now consider what it is that makes the values you circled (and those you added in the spaces above) so important to you. Record your thoughts below.

My Core Life Values List

VALUE: _____

WHY IT IS IMPORTANT TO ME:

_____

_____

_____

_____

VALUE: _____

WHY IT IS IMPORTANT TO ME:

_____

_____

_____

_____

VALUE: _____

WHY IT IS IMPORTANT TO ME:

_____

_____

_____

_____

VALUE: _____

WHY IT IS IMPORTANT TO ME:

_____

_____

_____

_____

VALUE: _____

WHY IT IS IMPORTANT TO ME:

_____

_____

_____

_____

VALUE: _____

WHY IT IS IMPORTANT TO ME:

_____

_____

_____

_____

VALUE: _____

WHY IT IS IMPORTANT TO ME:

_____

_____

_____

_____

VALUE: _____

WHY IT IS IMPORTANT TO ME:

_____

_____

_____

_____

VALUE: _____

WHY IT IS IMPORTANT TO ME:

_____

_____

_____

_____

Step 3. Now rank order your core life values based on their relative importance to you. The value that is most important *to you* should be listed on the first line below, and the remainder of your core values should follow in order, just as in Exercise 4.1 for work-related values.

Most Important   _____

_____

_____

_____

_____

_____

_____

_____

_____

_____

_____

_____

Least Important   _____

Later we'll discuss the ways your values can be integrated with information about your personality, interests, skills, and experiences to help you make career decisions that count.

QUESTIONS FOR CRITICAL THOUGHT

1. Why is it important to consider your work-related and core life values when making career decisions?
2. What are some of the basic differences between work-related and core life values?
3. What types of work-related and core life values have you developed recently?

KEY CONCEPTS TO REMEMBER

- Values are the cement that binds our career interests and skills together.
- Core life values are the principles and beliefs that make you who you are.
- It is important to consider work-related and *core* life values when making career decisions.

What's Your Story?

All of the components we've discussed in previous chapters—personality type, interests, values, and experiences—come together to create a picture of who you are. Whereas career counselors in the past may have focused on only one or two of these components and advocated a system of simply matching individuals to careers, the ever-evolving world of work has encouraged more holistic ways of thinking about career paths.

Think about your favorite book or movie. A good story has a strong plot that keeps it moving. These are the aspects that you can share with other people . . . "this happened, then this happened, then this happened." Whether it is a book, movie, or other story that you are sharing with a friend, the plot—as you probably already know—is the essence of what happened. Obviously, your life story began many years ago. What you choose to tell people about your life experiences as a child, what high school was like, or how you chose a college can be considered the plot of your story up to this point in you life.

Now, think about your favorite book or movie again. The things that make a story so compelling are the themes that support the plot. These themes represent the story beneath the story, the "whys" that keep you discussing the story with friends or thinking about it as you drive home. Themes make us think about and give the story its meaning.

Mark Savickas, an author, career counselor, and career development theorist, believes that careers are personal plot lines in everyone's life story. He believes that individuals are responsible for exploring their life themes and deciding which story lines to incorporate into their continuing story. Rather than a series of career assessment scores summarizing who are you in a few numbers or codes, wouldn't you rather think of yourself as the hero of your own story?

Rather than a series of career assessment scores summarizing who you are in a few numbers or codes, wouldn't you rather think of yourself as the hero of your own story?

CASE STUDIES TO CONSIDER

Amber

Amber, a third-year college student, worked for several weeks with a career counselor and diligently completed every assessment the counselor asked her to complete. Amber reached a point where she was aware of her interests, personality type, skills, and values, and narrowed her choices down to three options, but she still felt stuck. Amber's counselor asked her to describe a significant event in her life. It took her a while to decide what she wanted to share, but she finally decided to talk about an incident from her early childhood. She remembered standing in line at the grocery store and being acutely aware that her mother was very uncomfortable. When the cashier was done processing the order, her mother reluctantly handed her a stack of food stamps. Amber said that her mother kept looking around to see who might be there to see her use the stamps, but even having strangers see her was humiliating enough. When Amber's counselor asked her why she thought that memory had popped into her head, Amber explained that she had not realized until then that her family was not financially stable. At the same time, she remembered wondering why her mother seemed so concerned about the opinion of others and felt bad about the amount of shame her mother was experiencing.

Amber's counselor asked her to summarize that brief story in one line, like a title. Amber called it "Mom is ashamed to use food stamps." Amber's counselor asked her whether she thought that incident had shaped her in any way, and Amber explained that she had always wanted to help people in a way that made them feel as good as they possibly could about their life situation. As Amber looked over her list of career choices and tried to figure out if any of them aligned with that goal, working as an attorney with low-income families seemed to be the most connected. As Amber identified one of her life themes, helping people with dignity, she was able to differentiate between careers that simply fit with her self-concept and careers that would be much more meaningful.

> *The more connected your plot is to your themes, the more successful and satisfying your career story will be.*

As you think about writing your personal narrative, you'll want to consider both the plot (your major, career, graduate school, etc.) and the underlying themes that will give your plot meaning. The more connected your plot is to your themes, the more successful and satisfying your career story will be.

Rather than jumping right into the middle of your story, the first exercise of the chapter, Exercise 5.1, will give you insight into the earliest chapters of your life.

EXERCISE 5.1   *WHERE DID I BEGIN?*

A. If you're going to write your life story, you'll have to spend some time thinking about the way your story began. For the purpose of this exercise, think back to the earliest time you can remember. Think of a particular incident and try to remember as much as you can about it. When it's fresh in your mind, use the following space to write out all of the details. Remember that your story is your own. You don't have to qualify or justify anything you write. Tell the story from beginning to end, noting how you felt, who you were with, where you were, and what happened. Provide as much detail as possible.

_____

_____

_____
_____
_____
_____
_____
_____
_____
_____
_____
_____
_____
_____
_____
_____
_____
_____
_____
_____
_____
_____
_____
_____
_____
_____
_____

(If you need additional space for your story, please attach extra pages.)

B. For the final step in this exercise, you'll need a highlighter pen. If you don't want to make marks on your original story, make a photocopy first. Using the highlighter, mark all of the adjectives and adverbs. Although you will want to mark the entire story, pay particular attention to the way you describe yourself, the situation, and those around you. When you've finished, transfer these highlights onto a list of descriptors. When you read through the list, can you find any themes or repeating patterns? How representative are these in your life? In other words, is this story isolated or does it seem to fit a pattern of how you've often felt or been treated in your life? Use this space to write down the top three to five themes of this story:

_____
_____

_____

_____

These themes are the important foundation for your life story. These might be good identity traits that you would like to fold into your story. On the other hand, they may be things you consider negative that you would like to "fix" or otherwise address in your story. For example, if your story captured a theme of feeling like an outsider, perhaps your new story should include a plot in which you work to find a place where you feel comfortable and included. Remember, as the author of your story, it is completely up to you where you want to the plot to go.

People have been discussing the merits of role models and mentoring for years now. What we often forget to think about are the underlying connections that help us feel drawn to our role models or feel admiration for them. This next exercise is designed to help you identify people and characters that you admire and how they should be included in your story.

EXERCISE 5.2   *SUPPORTING CAST*

A. First, think about a person that you admire a great deal. This can be someone you know personally or someone famous. Write a paragraph simply describing that person and his or her accomplishments. In a second paragraph, describe what you particularly admire about this person. Would you like to be like this person? Why? What qualities does he or she have that you would like to have as well?

_____

_____

_____

_____

_____

_____

_____

_____

_____

_____

_____

_____

_____

_____

_____

_____

_____

_____

_____

_____

_____

_____

_____

_____

(If you need additional space for your story, please attach extra pages.)

B. Second, think about your favorite fictional character. This can be someone from any source (e.g., book, movie, play). As with the previous section of this exercise, use the first paragraph to describe the character and the second to write about why you feel particularly drawn or connected to that character.

_____

_____

_____

_____

_____

_____

_____

_____

_____

_____

_____

_____

_____

_____

_____

_____

_____

_____

_____

_____

(If you need additional space for your story, please attach extra pages.)

C. Just as you did in Exercise 5.1, you'll need a highlighter pen to finish this exercise. If you don't want to make marks on your original story, make a photocopy first. Using the highlighter, mark all of the adjectives and adverbs. When you've finished, transfer these highlights to a list of descriptors. When you read through the list, can you find any themes or repeating patterns? How representative are these in your life? In other words, what characteristics of people and characters that you admire seem to keep emerging in your stories? Do any of them match with descriptors on your list from Exercise 5.1? Make sure to take particular note of descriptions that keep recurring for you. Those will certainly need to be included in your life story.

D. Use this space to write down the top three to five themes of this story:

_____

_____

_____

_____

_____

E. Usually people create stories that involve other characters. Even single-actor plays generally involve the person playing multiple characters. There are two aspects of your supporting cast that you will need to figure out. You will need to decide who should be included in your cast of characters and what role they will play in your career story.

In the following space, list all the important characters in your life. Be sure to include everyone from the people you interact with daily to those who may have only slight influence. Most of these roles have already been cast, but remember to include roles that may not yet be cast in your present life story but that you expect will eventually be cast, such as children, grandchildren, or significant others.

_____

_____

_____

_____

_____

_____

_____

_____

_____

_____

_____

_____

_____

_____

_____

_____

_____

_____

_____

_____

_____

_____

_____

_____

_____

_____

_____

(If you need additional space for your story, please attach extra pages.)

After you have your list of characters, write a few things about each person using the format that follows:

Name of character: _____

What is his or her professional identity? _____

What are the underlying themes of his or her personal story? _____

_____

_____

How will his or her themes interact with yours? In other words, have you inherited expectations or themes from someone else?

_____

_____

_____

What will your story mean to this person? As you create your career narrative, how much impact will your decision have on this person?

_____

_____

_____

On a scale of 1–10, with 10 being the highest, how much influence will this person have on the authoring of your life story? _____

Will they be an advisor, an editor, or a coauthor? How do you feel about that? _____

_____

_____

Name of character: _____

What is his or her professional identity?

What are the underlying themes of his or her personal story?

_____

_____

How will his or her themes interact with yours? In other words, have you inherited expectations or themes from someone else?

_____

_____

_____

What will your story mean to this person? As you create your career narrative, how much impact will your decision have on this person?

_____

_____

_____

On a scale of 1–10, with 10 being the highest, how much influence will this person have on the authoring of your life story? _____

Will they be an advisor, an editor, or a coauthor? How do you feel about that? _____

_____

_____

Name of character: _____

What is his or her professional identity? _____

What are the underlying themes of his or her personal story? _____

_____

_____

How will his or her themes interact with yours? In other words, have you inherited expectations or themes from someone else?

_____

_____

_____

What will your story mean to this person? As you create your career narrative, how much impact will your decision have on this person?

_____

_____

_____

On a scale of 1–10, with 10 being the highest, how much influence will this person have on the authoring of your life story? _____

Will they be an advisor, an editor, or a coauthor? How do you feel about that? _____

_____

_____

Name of character: _____

What is his or her professional identity? _____

What are the underlying themes of his or her personal story? _____

_____

_____

How will his or her themes interact with yours? In other words, have you inherited expectations or themes from someone else?

_____

_____

_____

What will your story mean to this person? As you create your career narrative, how much impact will your decision have on this person?

_____

_____

_____

On a scale of 1–10, with 10 being the highest, how much influence will this person have on the authoring of your life story? _____

Will they be an advisor, an editor, or a coauthor? How do you feel about that? _____

_____

_____

Name of character: _____

What is his or her professional identity? _____

What are the underlying themes of his or her personal story? _____

_____

_____

How will his or her themes interact with yours? In other words, have you inherited expectations or themes from someone else?

_____

_____

_____

What will your story mean to this person? As you create your career narrative, how much impact will your decision have on this person?

_____

_____

_____

On a scale of 1–10, with 10 being the highest, how much influence will this person have on the authoring of your life story? _____

Will they be an advisor, an editor, or a coauthor? How do you feel about that? _____

_____

_____

As you go through this process, you'll be deciding who you want to be central characters and who you want to be peripheral characters. This will influence how you write your story and the content of it.

CASE STUDIES TO CONSIDER

Kira

Kira was encouraged to go to her college career center by her mother, who had met some career counselors during her visit to the "family weekend" on campus. Kira was a freshman with no idea what to major in and no real desire to decide. Kira was bright, articulate, and funny, and she was thoroughly enjoying her first year of school. When the counselor asked why she had decided to come to counseling, she rolled her eyes and said honestly that she had come only to please her mother. The counselor laughed and replied that while many students were "encouraged" to come for career counseling, not many actually did. In response, Kira started talking about her mother. She spoke about her mother's strength, courage, and dedication in raising Kira after her father left. Although her mother had never attended college, she had always just assumed Kira would go and had always saved money to make that possible. At the same time, Kira admired her mother's sense of humor and positive disposition in spite of all of the hardships she had encountered. While listening to Kira's story, her counselor began to make a list of all of the words Kira had used to describe her mother (strong, courageous, dedicated, sacrificing, funny, positive) and asked if those words also described Kira. She thought about that for a minute and agreed those were things she would like to be. The counselor then asked if it made sense for her to look for a career that would benefit from and encourage those themes to play out in her life. She agreed and became very enthusiastic about the search for that path. She used that energy to complete many activities that eventually led her to explore the field of education more closely. Kira took a part-time position with the admissions department on campus while she was in school and was offered a full-time position after she graduated. In her role, she worked with high school students and counselors to help them overcome obstacles in continuing their education.

By following the chapters in this book so far, you've explored, elaborated, and created numerous aspects of your story. As you continue to author the next chapter in your life, you'll need to start integrating the various pieces. Hopefully you've begun to see themes emerging that cross the different activities. In order to determine where the plot is heading, you'll need to tie these themes together. The next chapter will help you do that.

QUESTIONS FOR CRITICAL THOUGHT

1. What themes do you consider central to your life and who you are?
2. Who are the important people in your life who will impact your career story?
3. How will you take responsibility for authoring your future life story?

KEY CONCEPTS TO REMEMBER

- Your life is a story, and you are the hero. You are responsible for writing that story, including which themes to include, which characters will play a role, and how the plot will progress from here.
- Like any great adventure, your career story will have twists and turns. Good things as well as bad things will happen, and how you respond to those plot twists will help shape who you are.

Making the Pieces Fit

T This chapter will help you narrow your list of career possibilities to those that most closely match your personality, interests, abilities, experiences, values, and personal career narrative. In many ways, this is the core chapter of the book. It is the chapter in which most of your hard work and dedication to the career decision-making process will begin to pay off. This chapter begins to tie together the information you've been gathering and the increased knowledge you now have about yourself as they relate to making a career decision.

In Chapter 1, you learned about Super's theory of career development and the five stages of the career decision-making process: growth, exploration, establishment, maintenance, and disengagement. In Chapters 2, 3, 4, and 5, we examined the importance of personality, interests, abilities, experiences, values, and themes in career decision making. You completed several assessments and exercises to increase your awareness of what makes you a unique individual.

Hopefully you're beginning to get a better sense of what Super meant by the term self-concept. Your personal understanding of who you are—of your likes and dislikes, your skills and weaknesses, your experiences and values—is what determines your self-concept. You are the best judge of what you enjoy doing and, as such, are the world's greatest expert when it comes to making your career decisions.

The purpose of this chapter is to help you begin to integrate information about your personality, interests, abilities, experiences,

You are the best judge of what you enjoy doing and, as such, are the world's greatest expert when it comes to making your career decisions.

values, and life themes so that you'll be better prepared to make decisions about your career. You'll learn how to evaluate your responses to the exercises in earlier chapters as you begin to narrow your career possibilities. In the chapters that follow you'll select four or five careers to explore in more depth.

DEFINING MEANING AND PURPOSE

Just as the world of work changes constantly, you will continue to change and develop over your lifetime.

Just as the world of work changes constantly, you will continue to change and develop over your lifetime. Some elements of your self-concept will remain constant, some elements will be added, and some will become less important. The process of finding meaningful work includes deciding which elements or pieces of yourself you will express at work. If work is the way in which most of us connect with the world outside of our homes and families, how will you decide to frame that interaction for yourself?

As you approach career transitions, it is important to examine your self-concept and define your meaning and purpose globally as well as with your current decision. Once you have defined your current meaning and purpose, you can better analyze how your current decision aligns with your goals. Although many people find employment that closely aligns with their purpose, some seek employment that will allow them to fulfill their life purpose outside of work. For example, some people may seek employment with flexible hours so as to fulfill their personal goal of spending more time with their children or elderly parents. How you want to express your meaning and purpose is entirely up to you. The first step is to help you define it.

The following activities are designed to get you thinking about your own meaning and purpose. Remember that this is a tentative statement that will grow and change with you. In fact, what feels like a good fit today may seem off a little bit by tomorrow. The content itself is not as important as learning how to synthesize your goals into useful benchmarks to help in your decision-making. As author Nancy Thayer noted, "It's never too late . . . in life as in fiction . . . to revise."

EXERCISE 6.1	*WRITING A STATEMENT OF MEANING AND PURPOSE*

A. Now is the time to synthesize all of the information you've been gathering and processing throughout this book. Scan back through each of the activities you have completed and make a list of the components that particularly resonate with you. Pay attention to attributes that define you, what you stand for, what contributions or gifts you want to share with the world, and how you would like to prioritize your life. List those defining attributes here:

_____

_____

_____

_____

_____

_____

_____

_____

B. Narrow down your list to 5–6 key components that you would like to prioritize in this particular career transition.

_____

_____

_____

_____

_____

C. Take each of these components and create a statement beginning with the phrase "I will . . ." For example, someone who prioritizes the environment might include a statement like, "I will work in such a way that I can care for the planet." Write those statements here:

_____

_____

_____

_____

_____

D. Finally, look at this list of goal statements and see if you can construct a statement that captures a more general theme. Just like a corporate mission statement, this should summarize your _current_ thoughts on who you are and how you want to contribute to the world.

_____

_____

_____

_____

Your statement of mission and purpose should be able to help you in your career decision making. If you feel comfortable, share your statement with significant people in your life and ask them for feedback. Your statement should always be in draft form, constantly being revised as you experience new things. If you're living, you're changing, and your statement of purpose should change with you.

MATCHING SELF-CONCEPTS WITH WORK ENVIRONMENTS

Dr. Anne Roe developed a well-known system for classifying work environments in the 1950s when she became concerned that existing classification systems were inadequate. She was troubled that none of the classifications of occupations available at that time seemed to follow a logical framework of organization. Based on years of research and experience, Roe developed a classification system that includes eight occupational groups and work environments.

Service

This work environment involves serving and attending to the personal tastes, needs, and welfare of others. The focus is on doing something to help other people. Examples of occupations that fall into this work environment include social work, counseling, and many domestic and protective services, such as law enforcement and fire protection services.

Business Contact

The occupations included in this work environment involve the face-to-face sale of material goods or services. As in the Service category, person-to-person relationships are important, but in the Business Contact area these relationships are focused on persuading other people to engage in a particular course of action—such as buying a product—rather than on helping others. Examples of careers that fall into this work category include sales, public relations, marketing, advertising, and real estate.

Organization

This work environment is concerned primarily with the organization and efficient functioning of commercial enterprises and government activities where the quality of person-to-person relationships is more formalized. Managerial and administrative careers in business, industry, and government are included in this work environment. Examples of people in this area include small-business owners, accountants, hotel managers, and bankers.

Technology

The Technology work environment focuses on the production, maintenance, and transportation of commodities and utilities. Interpersonal relationships are of relatively little value. Instead, the focus is on dealing with *things* as opposed to dealing with *people*. Careers in engineering, machine trades, and the transportation industry belong in this environment. Examples include mechanic, carpenter, aerospace engineer, electrician, and construction worker.

Outdoors

This occupational group includes careers primarily concerned with the cultivation, preservation, and gathering of natural resources and animal welfare. As in the Technology work environment, many Outdoors careers provide few opportunities for emphasizing interpersonal relationships. Examples of Outdoors careers include landscape architects, forest rangers, horticulturists, tree surgeons, and gardeners.

Science

Science-related careers include occupations primarily concerned with scientific theory and its application to real-world problems. Medical doctors, physicists, research psychologists, university professors, and chiropractors are among the many professionals who are directly associated with this work environment.

General Culture

The General Culture category involves careers that are primarily concerned with the preservation and transmission of the general culture and heritage. The emphasis in this type of work environment is on human activities collectively rather than on individual person-to-person relationships. This group includes occupations in education, journalism, law, and careers that fall into a category often referred to as "the humanities." Examples of careers that fall into the General Culture category include school teacher, reporter, historian, lawyer, and newscaster.

Arts and Entertainment

Occupations included in this work environment involve the use of special skills in the creative arts and the world of entertainment. In this category, the focus is on a relationship between one person (or an organized group) and the general public. A wide range of careers falls into the Arts and Entertainment work environment, including examples such as designers and interior decorators, professional athletes, actors, musicians, and screenwriters.

To help you get a better sense of Roe's classification system, Table 6.1 summarizes the eight work environments.

Like many other career counselors, Roe believed that our job satisfaction, career success, and on-the-job performance are directly related to the match between our self-concept and our work environment. Dr. John Holland, the vocational psychologist referred to back in Chapter 3, calls this match **congruence**. Holland believed that individuals with high levels of congruence will be more satisfied with their careers, will achieve greater success within their occupations, and will remain in their careers over a longer period. Persons with low levels of congruence, on the other

TABLE 6.1	*Summary of work environments.*	
WORK ENVIRONMENT	**SAMPLE OCCUPATIONS**	**CHARACTERISTICS OF PEOPLE WHO LIKE WORKING IN THESE ENVIRONMENTS**
Service	Social worker, police officer, family counselor, occupational therapist	Enjoy serving and attending to the personal tastes, needs, and welfare of other people; obtain a strong sense of satisfaction from helping and/or protecting other people.
Business Contact	Real estate agent, salesperson, insurance agent, public relations specialist	Enjoy persuading other people to engage in a particular course of action, such as the purchase of a commodity or service.
Organization	Employment manager, human resources director, business executive, small-business owner	Enjoy engaging in tasks that involve a high level of organization and precision; often satisfied by supervising or managing others.
Technology	Repair person, mechanic, civil engineer, carpenter	Enjoy producing, transporting, and/or fixing things; more satisfied working with tools and objects than with people.
Outdoors	Forest ranger, horticulturalist, wildlife specialist, farmer	Enjoy working in outdoor settings; often favor working with animals and plants rather than with people.
Science	chiropractor, X-ray technician, dentist, pediatrician	Enjoy working with scientific theory and its application to real-world problems.
General Culture	Lawyer, high school teacher, librarian, historian	Enjoy interacting with groups of people in an effort to preserve and/or transmit knowledge and cultural heritage.
Arts and Entertainment	Interior decorator, artist, professional athlete, actor	Enjoy environments that provide opportunities for artistic expression and/or the use of special skills in an entertainment industry.

hand, are likely to experience job dissatisfaction and relatively poor on-the-job performance. As a result, persons who are not in congruent work environments are likely to search for different employment opportunities (and sometimes new careers altogether).

CASE STUDIES TO CONSIDER

Chandra

To illustrate the concept of congruence, let's turn to Chandra, a senior attending a college on the West Coast. Chandra was about to graduate with a degree in mechanical engineering. When one of Chandra's friends asked her if she was excited to be graduating, she said rather emphatically, "No!" When Chandra's career counselor asked her to explain her answer, Chandra talked about the many challenges she faced during college.

During her first year, Chandra found that she struggled a great deal when it came to writing assignments. She had a very hard time preparing research papers and found it extremely difficult to answer essay questions on tests. She just couldn't seem to get her thoughts down on paper very easily.

In her sophomore year Chandra discovered that she had a learning disability. After meeting with the director of Special Student Services on campus, Chandra began to work through the challenges posed by her disability. She took advantage of the tutoring services available at the university and worked with her instructors to make sure appropriate accommodations were available in each of her classes. As a result, Chandra was able to overcome the challenges posed by her disability and performed very well in her more demanding engineering courses.

Despite the appearance that all was well, however, Chandra was not looking forward to graduation. She was anxious and fearful about beginning her career as an engineer. As she explored with her counselor possible reasons for her feelings, it became apparent that Chandra's anxieties were due to one simple fact: She didn't like engineering! After four years of classes and even an internship in mechanical engineering, Chandra had come to realize that a career in engineering wasn't such a good choice after all.

As Chandra discussed her situation, her counselor worked with her to help her clarify the reasons why engineering wasn't as appealing as she thought it would be. When Chandra's counselor asked her to explain the work environment of an engineer, the types of activities that she enjoyed, the range of abilities that she had, and the things that mattered most to her in life, it didn't take long for Chandra to realize why a career in engineering wasn't all that appealing.

Chandra had been preparing for a career characterized in Roe's classification system as a Technical working environment. Mechanical engineers work with their hands a great deal, in a routine, organized setting with relatively little face-to-face contact with other people. Yet based on her self-concept (i.e., her understanding of her personality, her likes and interests, her skills and talents, and her values and beliefs), it was clear that Chandra was more Service oriented.

She loved to be around large groups of people. She enjoyed the opportunity to teach others and help them find solutions to their problems. She preferred working with people rather than with things, and she placed a high value on work that provided lots of opportunity to interact with others. For Chandra, a career as a mechanical engineer wasn't a very good match. A social service career would probably be much more fulfilling. Consequently, Chandra began to explore possible careers in fields such as social work and counseling. Today, Chandra is the director of a women's shelter in Atlanta and thoroughly enjoys her career.

The challenge is to seek career opportunities that will maximize your chances of establishing a high level of congruence between your career self-concept and your work environment, which brings us to the next stage in the process. It's time to integrate the results of the exercises you completed in previous chapters and compare them with the world of work. Doing so will help you identify work environments that are likely to provide you with job satisfaction, career stability, and on-the-job success.

For some people, brief descriptions of the eight work environments (such as those provided in Table 6.1) are all that's needed to identify careers likely to provide satisfaction, stability, and success. But assessments similar to those that you completed in previous chapters provide additional information that almost always helps increase the overall effectiveness of a career decision.

As you complete the exercises in this chapter, you may find that the results of previous exercises validate a career choice you've already been considering. Or you may discover that the exercises helped you learn about aspects of yourself that you weren't aware of before. Either way, you're likely to discover that by completing these exercises you'll increase your awareness of your self-concept and enhance your ability to select the best type of work environment for *you*.

The challenge is to seek career opportunities that will maximize your chances of establishing a high level of congruence between your career self-concept and your work environment.

FINDING YOUR WORK ENVIRONMENT	**EXERCISE 6.2**

Begin by scoring the exercises that you've already completed in this book. To complete this process, remove Appendix B from the back of the book and follow the scoring directions.

For each of the exercises that you score, you'll have a point value corresponding to each of the eight career types. Fill in those values in the spaces below.

Once you've recorded your scores for each exercise, compute your total scores for each career type by summing the scores for all five exercises.

SCORES FROM EXERCISE 2.1

Service	Business Contact	Organization	Technology	Outdoors	Science	General Culture	Arts & Entertainment
___	___	___	___	___	___	___	___

SCORES FROM EXERCISE 3.2

Service	Business Contact	Organization	Technology	Outdoors	Science	General Culture	Arts & Entertainment
___	___	___	___	___	___	___	___

SCORES FROM EXERCISE 3.3

Service	Business Contact	Organization	Technology	Outdoors	Science	General Culture	Arts & Entertainment
___	___	___	___	___	___	___	___

SCORES FROM EXERCISE 3.4

Service	Business Contact	Organization	Technology	Outdoors	Science	General Culture	Arts & Entertainment
___	___	___	___	___	___	___	___

SCORES FROM EXERCISE 3.5

Service	Business Contact	Organization	Technology	Outdoors	Science	General Culture	Arts & Entertainment
___	___	___	___	___	___	___	___

TOTAL SCORES (ADD THE SCORES IN THE COLUMNS ABOVE)

Service	Business Contact	Organization	Technology	Outdoors	Science	General Culture	Arts & Entertainment
___	___	___	___	___	___	___	___

Because the total scores are the combined results from the assessments you've already completed, they include aspects of your personality, interests, skills, and experiences. The results can help you narrow your list of career possibilities.

Write in the three career types for which your total scores were the highest:

1. _____
2. _____
3. _____

Your primary "career type" is the category for which your score is the highest. Your secondary career type is the category for which your score is the second highest. Your tertiary, or third level, career type is the category for which your score is the third highest. If the scores for two of your types are identical, then your career type is probably best described as a combination of those two types.

IDENTIFYING CAREERS THAT MATCH YOUR CAREER TYPE

Now that you have a good idea what your primary career type is, it will be helpful for you to take a look at careers that are congruent with that type. You can begin this process by skimming through the career lists in Appendix C.

As you review the lists, make a note of those careers that pique your interest. Many of the careers listed in Appendix C may not be all that interesting to you, even though they correspond with your primary career type. That's actually very common. However, odds are that you'll find some of them rather interesting and, therefore, worthy of further exploration.

If your primary career type as revealed in Exercise 6.2 is several points higher than any of the other types, then you may want to focus your attention at this point on careers that correspond only with your primary type. If, however, the results of Exercise 6.2 revealed career types whose point totals were rather close to one another, then you might want to take a look at the careers listed in several of the career areas listed in Appendix C.

Make a list below of all careers that you're interested in pursuing further. Don't limit yourself to those careers listed in Appendix C that correspond with your career type. Also consider other careers of interest, such as those listed on an interest inventory score report, ones that you have identified as part of your career story, or other careers you have in mind.

LIST OF INTERESTING CAREERS

_____
_____
_____
_____
_____
_____
_____
_____
_____
_____

In order to complete some of the exercises in the remaining chapters, you're going to need to narrow your list of career options to the four or five that interest you the most. For some folks this is a rather easy task, but for others it can be a much more difficult enterprise. Use the statement of meaning and purpose that you developed earlier in the chapter to compare and then narrow down your list of career options by moving careers that are congruent or closely fit with your statement of purpose up toward the top the list.

CASE STUDIES IN NARROWING CAREER OPTIONS

CASE STUDIES TO CONSIDER

Mario and Meredith

Mario, a first-year college student, completed an interest inventory and a skills assessment. His results indicated that Mario possessed an Arts and Entertainment career type. He consulted Appendix C for a listing of occupations corresponding to the Arts and Entertainment work environment. Many of those careers were ones that he had considered at different times.

Mario knew he wanted to pursue a career that would involve creative expression as well as autonomy, but he also wanted a career that would provide a stable income. He had an actor friend who often went four or five months without work, and that simply wasn't something Mario was willing to do; he wanted the safety and security of a regular paycheck. Although his longer list of career possibilities included freelance artist and actor, Mario selected careers in interior design and commercial art to explore in more detail. Today, Mario is the successful co-owner of an interior design firm in Connecticut.

Meredith's situation was somewhat different from Mario's. She had a difficult time generating even a list of initial career options. Like Mario, Meredith had taken lots of different classes in college, but none of them seemed to stand out as any more interesting than the others.

The results of Meredith's interest inventory and skills assessments helped her understand why she was having such a difficult time narrowing down career options: Her primary and secondary career types were nearly identical in value. When she completed Exercise 6.2, she discovered that Arts and Entertainment and Service career types were only two points different from each other. In essence, Meredith's career type was a combination of the two.

When it came time to examine lists of careers, Meredith looked at both the Arts and Entertainment and Service occupation groupings. What resulted was a list of 18 occupations that she thought might be worth pursuing. When it came time to narrow the list to four or five, Meredith decided to consider the educational requirements associated with each career.

Meredith was a single mother with two children. She didn't want to select a career that would require several years of graduate school—at least not for now. That and her consideration of the earning potential of each career helped her narrow down her options. Her resulting list of career possibilities included social worker, art teacher, and addictions counselor. Eventually, Meredith became an art teacher and has been enjoying her career as a teacher for the past 12 years.

Whether your situation is more like Mario's or Meredith's, one thing is for sure: The information you've been gathering about the world of work and the increased awareness you have about your self-concept will help you a great deal as you narrow your list of potential careers down to four or five worthy of continued exploration.

Perhaps the most important things to keep in mind are your work-related and core life values. As you narrow your list of options, it's very important to think about pursuing careers congruent with your values and themes. If you're like most people, you certainly don't want to engage in a thorough exploration of a career that's going to conflict with many of your work and life values. Before completing Exercise 6.3, "Narrowing Your Career Options," you should review the values lists you generated back in Chapter 4 and the list of important story themes from Chapter 5.

EXERCISE 6.4   *NARROWING YOUR CAREER OPTIONS*

Based on the review of your values lists and the preliminary career choices you identified in Exercise 6.2, narrow your career possibilities to the four or five options that seem most worthy of continued exploration and list them here.

CAREER OPTIONS TO EXPLORE FURTHER

1. _____

2. _____

3. _____

4. _____

5. _____

We'll refer to this list in subsequent chapters as we discuss specific techniques for exploring career options.

QUESTIONS FOR CRITICAL THOUGHT

1. What are some of the most important lessons you've learned about making career decisions from the first six chapters of the book?
2. Why do you suppose that *you* are the world's greatest expert when it comes to making *your* career decisions?
3. Why do you think that job satisfaction, career stability, and on-the-job success are all related to the degree to which your work environment and your career self-concept are congruent?
4. Why is it that so many adults end up working in environments that aren't congruent with their personality, interests, skills, or values?

KEY CONCEPTS TO CONSIDER

- Your job satisfaction, career stability, and on-the-job performance depend on the match between your self-concept and your work environment.
- Think about pursuing careers that are congruent with your values and life themes.

Navigating the Maze

METHODS OF CAREER EXPLORATION

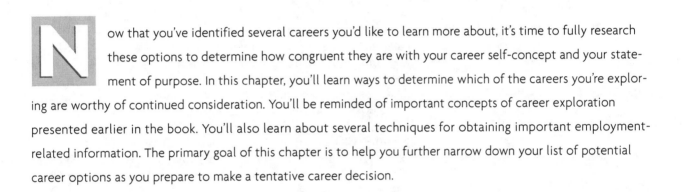

Now that you've identified several careers you'd like to learn more about, it's time to fully research these options to determine how congruent they are with your career self-concept and your statement of purpose. In this chapter, you'll learn ways to determine which of the careers you're exploring are worthy of continued consideration. You'll be reminded of important concepts of career exploration presented earlier in the book. You'll also learn about several techniques for obtaining important employment-related information. The primary goal of this chapter is to help you further narrow down your list of potential career options as you prepare to make a tentative career decision.

A REVIEW OF THE CAREER EXPLORATION PROCESS

You may recall from Chapter 1 that Super referred to the second phase of the career decision-making process as *exploration*. In Chapters 2, 3, 4, and 5 you engaged in activities related to the *crystallizing* stage of *exploration*. You began by thinking about some of your career dreams and childhood aspirations.

Then you completed exercises designed to increase your understanding and awareness of your personality, interests, skills, experiences, values, and life themes. At the end of Chapter 6 you narrowed your original list of career options down to four or five to explore in more detail.

Now it's time to embark on the *specifying* substage of career exploration. You'll make some critical decisions about whether to pursue a particular career or not. Each exercise completed during this stage of the career decision-making process will require you to do some important research.

DEVELOPING A SYSTEM OF INFORMATION GATHERING

The first and most important activity that you'll engage in during this stage of career development is information gathering. Numerous sources of information about careers are available to you. As you consider various career fields and specific occupations within those fields, you will want to keep the information you've gathered organized and readily accessible. Start by creating an individual file for each of the occupations included in your "short list" of career possibilities. File information about your career possibilities as you go to keep from getting overwhelmed.

WORLD OF WORK: FORECASTS AND TRENDS

In addition to learning about ways to classify work environments, making effective career decisions also requires you to increase your awareness of trends and forecasts regarding the world of work. In recent years, many people have predicted the economic and demographic employment trends of the 21st century. Some of their predictions have been no more accurate than a daily horoscope reading. Others, however, have provided important information that can be very useful as you consider career opportunities.

One of the best things you can do at this point is get in the habit of going to the library or accessing the Internet to read about the world of work and gain a better idea of career projections. Just as you might window shop to check out the latest fashions, skimming through up-to-date occupational information and economic projections will give you a clearer picture of the world of work.

Just as you might window shop to check out the latest fashions, skimming through up-to-date occupational information and economic projections will give you a clearer picture of the world of work.

It will be important for you to gather various types of information during *all* stages of your career decision-making process. Fortunately, numerous sources are available for increasing your understanding of work trends. Among these resources are best-selling books and popular magazines, which often contain useful articles and feature stories related to the world of work. Obtaining accurate, up-to-date information about employment opportunities will be important as you continue to make career decisions. In fact, keeping a close watch on employment trends and changes in the world of work may be the key to your personal career satisfaction and success.

One way to find out about current information is to read magazines, such as *Money* or *Fortune,* that are primarily devoted to covering labor issues. These types of magazines often include feature articles devoted to employment issues and job projections. Even weekly and monthly news magazines, such as *Time, Newsweek,* and *U.S. News & World Report,* can supply you with important information about the world of work.

As you begin to gather information, you might also be surprised at how helpful some newspapers can be. Larger newspapers, such as the *Wall Street Journal, USA Today,* and the *New York Times,* usually include stories related to the world of work. Your local newspaper might be informative as well, particularly about employment opportunities in industries located in your community.

Another quick and easy way to find out what categories of careers are on the rise is to see what types of training programs are being offered at your community college or adult education center. The courses and programs that are popular at a community college or adult education center often reflect the skills that employers in that region are looking for.

U.S. Department of Labor Information

A host of resources are specifically designed for the information-gathering stage of career development. The following paragraphs describe these valuable resources in more detail.

Occupational Outlook Handbook

The *Occupational Outlook Handbook (OOH)* is published every two years by the U.S. Department of Labor's Bureau of Labor Statistics. Each issue of the handbook includes hundreds of occupations. For each one you will find a description of the nature of the work, general working conditions, expected earnings, educational and training qualifications, opportunities for advancement, and a five-year employment outlook.

The *OOH* also includes a listing of sources of additional information about a particular career. The print version of the *OOH* is available at most libraries, but the easiest way to access the information is using the Web site at http://www.bls.gov/oco/home.htm. You can use the Web site in a number of ways. First, you can use the search function to look for a specific topic or occupational title. Second, you can browse by particular occupational groups such as management, production, or service. Third, you can view all occupations in alphabetical order. The *OOH* also provides job search tips, links to information about the job market by state, and much more.

See Figure 7.1 for an example of an *OOH* entry.

FIGURE 7.1

PSYCHOLOGISTS

(O*NET   19-3031.01,   19-3031.02,   19-3031.03,   19-3032.00, 19-3039.99)

Significant Points

- About 4 out of 10 psychologists are self-employed, compared with less than 1 out of 10 among all professional workers.

- Most specialists, including clinical and counseling psychologists, need a doctoral degree; school psychologists need an educational specialist degree, and industrial-organizational psychologists need a master's degree.

- Competition for admission to graduate psychology programs is keen.

- Overall employment of psychologists is expected to grow faster than the average for all occupations through 2014.

Nature of the Work

Psychologists study the human mind and human behavior. Research psychologists investigate the physical, cognitive, emotional, or social aspects of human behavior. Psychologists in health service provider fields provide mental health care in hospitals, clinics, schools, or private settings. Psychologists employed in applied settings, such as business, industry, government, or nonprofits, provide training, conduct research, design systems, and act as advocates for psychology.

Like other social scientists, psychologists formulate hypotheses and collect data to test their validity. Research methods vary with the topic under study. Psychologists sometimes gather information through controlled laboratory experiments or by administering personality, performance, aptitude, or intelligence tests. Other methods include observation, interviews, questionnaires, clinical studies, and surveys.

Psychologists apply their knowledge to a wide range of endeavors, including health and human services, management, education, law, and sports. In addition to working in a variety of settings, psychologists usually specialize in one of a number of different areas.

Clinical psychologists—who constitute the largest specialty—work most often in counseling centers, independent or group practices, hospitals, or clinics. They help mentally and emotionally disturbed clients adjust to life and may assist medical and surgical patients in dealing with illnesses or injuries. Some clinical psychologists work in physical rehabilitation settings, treating patients with spinal cord injuries, chronic pain or illness, stroke, arthritis, and neurological conditions. Others help people deal with times of personal crisis, such as divorce or the death of a loved one.

Clinical psychologists often interview patients and give diagnostic tests. They may provide individual, family, or group psychotherapy and may design and implement behavior modification programs. Some clinical psychologists collaborate with physicians and other specialists to develop and implement treatment and intervention programs that patients can understand and comply with. Other clinical psychologists work in universities and medical schools, where they train graduate students in the delivery of mental health and behavioral medicine services. Some administer community mental health programs.

Areas of specialization within clinical psychology include health psychology, neuropsychology, and geropsychology. *Health psychologists* promote good health through health maintenance counseling programs designed to help people achieve goals, such as stopping smoking or losing weight. *Neuropsychologists* study the relation between the brain and behavior. They often work in stroke and head injury programs. *Geropsychologists* deal with the special problems faced by the elderly, The emergence and growth of these specialties reflects the increasing participation of psychologists in providing direct services to special patient populations.

Often, clinical psychologists will consult with other medical personnel regarding the best treatment for patients, especially treatment that includes medication. Clinical psychologists generally are not permitted to prescribe medication to treat patients; only psychiatrists and other medical doctors may prescribe certain medications. (See the statement on physicians and surgeons elsewhere in the *Handbook*.) However, two States—Louisiana and New Mexico—currently allow clinical psychologists to prescribe medication with some limitations, and similar proposals have been made in other States.

Counseling psychologists use various techniques, including interviewing and testing, to advise people on how to deal with problems of everyday living. They work in settings such as university counseling centers, hospitals, and individual or group practices. (See also the statements on counselors and social workers elsewhere in the *Handbook*.)

School psychologists work with students in elementary and secondary schools. They collaborate with teachers, parents, and school personnel to create safe, healthy, and supportive learning environments for all students; address students' learning and behavior problems; improve classroom management strategies or parenting skills; counter substance abuse; assess students with learning disabilities and gifted and talented students to help determine the best way to educate them; and improve teaching, learning, and socialization strategies. They also may evaluate the effectiveness of academic programs, prevention programs, behavior management procedures, and other services provided in the school setting.

Industrial-organizational psychologists apply psychological principles and research methods to the workplace in the interest of improving productivity and the quality of worklife. They also are involved in research on management and marketing problems. They screen, train and counsel applicants for jobs, as well as perform organizational development and analysis. An industrial psychologist might work with management to reorganize the work setting in order to improve productivity or quality of life in the workplace. Industrial psychologists frequently act as consultants, brought in by management to solve a particular problem.

Developmental psychologists study the physiological, cognitive, and social development that takes place throughout life. Some specialize in behavior during infancy, childhood, and adolescence, or changes that occur during maturity or old age. Developmental psychologists also may study developmental disabilities and their effects. Increasingly, research is developing ways to help elderly people remain independent as long as possible.

Social psychologists examine people's interactions with others and with the social environment. They work in organizational consultation, marketing research, systems design, or other applied psychology fields. Prominent areas of study include group behavior, leadership, attitudes, and perception.

Experimental or *research psychologists* work in university and private research centers and in business, nonprofit, and governmental organizations. They study the behavior of both human beings and animals, such as rats, monkeys, and pigeons. Prominent areas of study in experimental research include motivation, thought, attention, learning and memory, sensory and perceptual processes, effects of substance abuse, and genetic and neurological factors affecting behavior.

Working Conditions

A psychologist's subfield and place of employment determine his or her working conditions. Clinical, school, and counseling psychologists in private practice have their own offices and set their own hours. However, they often offer evening and weekend hours to accommodate their clients. Those employed in hospitals, nursing homes, and other health care facilities may work shifts that include evenings and weekends, while those who work in schools and clinics generally work regular hours.

Psychologists employed as faculty by colleges and universities divide their time between teaching and research and also may have administrative responsibilities; many have part-time consulting practices. Most psychologists in government and industry have structured schedules.

Increasingly, many psychologists are working as part of a team, consulting with other psychologists and professionals. Many experience pressures because of deadlines, tight schedules, and overtime. Their routine may be interrupted frequently. Travel may be required in order to attend conferences or conduct research.

Training, Other Qualifications, and Advancement

A doctoral degree usually is required for employment as an independent licensed clinical or counseling psychologist. Psychologists with a Ph.D. qualify for a wide range of teaching, research, clinical, and counseling positions in universities, health care services, elementary and secondary schools, private industry, and government. Psychologists with a Doctor of Psychology (Psy.D.) degree usually work in clinical positions or in private practices, but they also sometime teach, conduct research, or carry out administrative responsibilities.

A doctoral degree generally requires 5 to 7 years of graduate study. The Ph.D. degree culminates in a dissertation based on original research. Courses in quantitative research methods, which include the use of computer-based analysis, are an integral part of graduate study and are necessary to complete the dissertation. The Psy.D. may be based on practical work and examinations rather than a dissertation. In clinical or counseling psychology, the requirements for the doctoral degree include at least a 1-year internship.

A specialist degree is required in most States for an individual to work as a school psychologist, although a few States still credential school psychologists with master's degrees. A specialist (Ed.S.) degree in school psychology requires a minimum of 3 years of full-time graduate study (at least 60 graduate semester hours) and a 1-year internship. Because their professional practice addresses educational and mental health components of students' development, school psychologists' training includes coursework in both education and psychology.

Persons with a master's degree in psychology may work as industrial-organizational psychologists. They also may work as psychological assistants under the supervision of doctoral-level psychologists and may conduct research or psychological evaluations. A master's degree in psychology requires at least 2 years of full-time graduate study. Requirements usually include practical experience in an applied setting and a master's thesis based on an original research project.

Competition for admission to graduate psychology programs is keen. Some universities require applicants to have an undergraduate major in psychology. Others prefer only coursework in basic psychology with courses in the biological, physical, and social sciences and in statistics and mathematics.

A bachelor's degree in psychology qualifies a person to assist psychologists and other professionals in community mental health centers, vocational rehabilitation offices, and correctional programs. Bachelor's degree holders may work as research or administrative assistants for psychologists. Some work as technicians in related fields, such as marketing research. Many find employment in other areas, such as sales or business management.

In the Federal Government, candidates having at least 24 semester hours in psychology and one course in statistics qualify for entry-level positions. However, competition for these jobs is keen because this is one of the few areas in which one can work as a psychologist without an advanced degree.

The American Psychological Association (APA) presently accredits doctoral training programs in clinical, counseling, and school psychology, as well as accrediting institutions that provide internships for doctoral students in school, clinical, and counseling psychology. The National Association of School Psychologists, with the assistance of the National Council for Accreditation of Teacher Education, also is involved in the accreditation of advanced degree programs in school psychology.

Psychologists in independent practice or those who offer any type of patient care—including clinical, counseling, and school psychologists—must meet certification or licensing requirements in all States and the District of Columbia. Licensing laws vary by State and by type of position and require licensed or certified psychologists to limit their practice to areas in which they have developed professional competence through training and experience. Clinical and counseling psychologists usually require a doctorate in psychology, the completion of an approved internship, and 1 to 2 years of professional experience. In addition, all States require that applicants pass an examination. Most State licensing boards administer a standardized test, and many supplement that with additional oral or essay questions. Some States require continuing education for renewal of the license.

The National Association of School Psychologists (NASP) awards the Nationally Certified School Psychologist (NCSP) designation, which recognizes professional competency in school psychology at a national, rather than State, level. Currently, 26 States recognize the NCSP and allow those with the certification to transfer credentials from one State to another without taking a new certification exam. In States that recognize the NCSP, the requirements for certification or licensure and those for the NCSP often are the same or similar. Requirements for the NCSP include the completion of 60 graduate semester hours in school psychology; a 1,200-hour internship, 600 hours of which must be completed in a school setting; and a passing score on the National School Psychology Examination.

The American Board of Professional Psychology (ABPP) recognizes professional achievement by awarding specialty certification, primarily in clinical psychology, clinical neuropsychology, and counseling, forensic, industrial-organizational, and school psychology. Candidates for ABPP certification need a doctorate in psychology, postdoctoral training in their specialty, five years of experience, professional endorsements, and a passing grade on an examination.

Aspiring psychologists who are interested in direct patient care must be emotionally stable, mature, and able to deal effectively with people. Sensitivity, compassion, good communication skills, and the ability to lead and inspire others are particularly important qualities for persons wishing to do clinical work and counseling. Research psychologists should be able to do detailed work both independently and as part of a team. Patience and perseverance are vital qualities, because achieving results in the psychological treatment of patients or in research may take a long time.

Employment

Psychologists held about 179,000 jobs in 2004. Educational institutions employed about 1 out of 4 psychologists in positions other than teaching, such as counseling, testing, research, and administration. Almost 2 out of 10 were employed in health care, primarily in offices of mental health practitioners, physicians' offices, outpatient mental health and substance abuse centers, and private hospitals. Government agencies at the State and local levels employed psychologists in public hospitals, clinics, correctional facilities, and other settings.

After several years of experience, some psychologists—usually those with doctoral degrees—enter private practice or set up private research or consulting firms. About 4 out of 10 psychologists were self-employed in 2004, compared with less than 1 out of 10 among all professional workers.

In addition to the previously mentioned jobs, many psychologists held faculty positions at colleges and universities and as high school psychology teachers. (See the statements on teachers—postsecondary and teachers—preschool, kindergarten, elementary, middle, and secondary elsewhere in the *Handbook*.)

Job Outlook

Employment of psychologists is expected to grow faster than the average for all occupations through 2014, because of increased demand for psychological services in schools, hospitals, social service agencies, mental health centers, substance abuse treatment clinics, consulting firms, and private companies.

Among the specialties in this field, school psychologists—especially those with a specialist degree or higher—may enjoy the best job opportunities. Growing awareness of how students' mental health and behavioral problems, such as bullying, affect learning is increasing demand for school psychologists to offer student counseling and mental health services. Clinical and counseling psychologists will be needed to help people deal with depression and other mental disorders, marriage and family problems, job stress, and addiction. The rise in health care costs associated with unhealthy lifestyles, such as smoking, alcoholism, and obesity, has made prevention and treatment more critical. An increase in the number of employee assistance programs, which help workers deal with personal problems, also should spur job growth in clinical and counseling specialties. Industrial-organizational psychologists will be in demand to help to boost worker productivity and retention rates in a wide range of businesses. Industrial-organizational psychologists will help companies deal with issues such as workplace diversity and antidiscrimination policies. Companies also will use psychologists' expertise in survey design, analysis, and research to develop tools for marketing evaluation and statistical analysis.

Demand should be particularly strong for persons holding doctorates from leading universities in applied specialties—such as counseling, health, and school psychology. Psychologists with extensive training in quantitative research methods and computer science may have a competitive edge over applicants without background.

Master's degree holders in fields other than industrial-organizational psychology will face keen competition for jobs, because of the limited number of positions that require only a master's degree. Master's degree holders may find jobs as psychological assistants or counselors, providing mental health services under the direct supervision of a licensed psychologist. Still others may find jobs involving research and data collection and analysis in universities, government, or private companies.

Opportunities directly related to psychology will be limited for bachelor's degree holders. Some may find jobs as assistants in rehabilitation centers or in other jobs involving data collection and analysis. Those who meet State certification requirements may become high school psychology teachers.

Earnings

Median annual earnings of wage and salary clinical, counseling, and school psychologists in May 2004 were $54,950. The middle 50 percent earned between $41,850 and $71,880. The lowest 10 percent earned less than $32,280, and the highest 10 percent earned more than $92,250. Median annual earnings in the industries employing the largest numbers of clinical, counseling, and school psychologists in May 2004 were:

Offices of other health practitioners.............	$64,460
Elementary and secondary schools...............	58,360
Outpatient care centers................................	46,850
Individual and family services.......................	42,640

Median annual earnings of wage and salary industrial-organizational psychologists in May 2004 were $71,400. The middle 50 percent earned between $56,880 and $93,210. The lowest 10 percent earned less than $45,620, and the highest 10 percent earned more than $125,560.

Related Occupations

Psychologists are trained to conduct research and teach, evaluate, counsel, and advise individuals and groups with special needs. Others who do this kind of work include clergy, counselors, physicians and surgeons, social workers, sociologists, and special education teachers.

Sources of Additional Information

For information on careers, educational requirements, financial assistance, and licensing in all fields of psychology, contact:

➢ American Psychological Association, Research Office and Education Directorate, 750 1st St. N.E., Washington, DC 20002-4242. Internet: http://www.apa.org/students

For information on careers, educational requirements, certification, and licensing of school psychologists, contact:

➢ National Association of School Psychologists, 4340 East West Hwy., Suite 402, Bethesda, MD 20814. Internet: http://www.nasponline.org

Information about State licensing requirements is available from:

➢ Association of State and Provincial Psychology Boards, P.O. Box 241245, Montgomery, AL 36124-1245. Internet: http://www.asppb.org

Information about psychology specialty certifications is available from:

➢ American Board of Professional Psychology, Inc., 300 Drayton St., 3rd Floor, Savannah, GA31401. Internet: http://www.abpp.org

Occupational Outlook Quarterly

The U.S. Department of Labor's Bureau of Labor Statistics also publishes the *Occupational Outlook Quarterly (OOQ)*. This publication, which is arranged much like a magazine, serves as an update to the *OOH*. Each edition includes additional information about many of the jobs listed in the *OOH*. These quarterly updates can help you obtain the most up-to-date information available about most careers. The *OOQ* can usually be found at institutions that also have access to the *OOH*. An online version of the *OOQ* is available at http://www.bls.gov/opub/ooq/ooqhome.htm.

O*NET

O*NET, the Occupational Information Network, is an easy-to-use database that you can access at http://online.onetcenter.org. O*NET contains comprehensive information on job requirements and worker competencies for more than 800 occupations. The information is continually updated with information provided by workers from each occupation. There are three basic ways to use O*NET to gather information. First, you can search occupations using keywords or by browsing categories. Second, you can have the system search for occupations based on skills you would like to use in your work. Third, if you have worked with a career counselor or instructor and know your *Dictionary of Occupational Titles, Military Occupational Classification, Standard Occupational Classification*, or *Classification of Instructional Programs* code, you can search for occupational titles by that code.

The O*NET Summary Report contains a wealth of information about occupations, including required tasks, tools and technology, knowledge, skills, abilities, work activities, work content, amount of preparation needed (job zone), interests, work styles, work values, related occupations, wages, employment outlook, and links to additional information.

Additional U.S. Department of Labor Publications

In addition to publishing the *OOH*, the *OOQ*, and O*NET, the U.S. Department of Labor also sponsors the publication of hundreds of other useful resources including the *Guide for Occupational Exploration* and the *Dictionary of Occupational Titles*. In addition, they offer specific documents, such as "Job Options for Women" and the "Job Guide for Young Workers," to name a few. These and other publications that address particular aspects of the world of work are available at most libraries. If you're unable to locate them, you can write to the Bureau of Labor Statistics, U.S. Department of Labor, Washington, DC 20212; call 202-219-7316, or go to http://www.bls.gov. The Bureau's Public Affairs Office will help you obtain information relevant to the careers you're pursuing.

Computerized Career Information and Guidance Programs

One of the best ways to locate information about occupations is to learn about and use computerized career information and guidance programs available through most college and university career centers. The more popular programs include the System of Interactive Guidance and Information (SIGIplus), Computerized Heuristic Occupational Information and Career Exploration System (CHOICES), DISCOVER, the Kuder Career Planning system, and state Career Information Systems (CIS). Most career centers offer these systems on computers in their resource centers or online using special log-in procedures. Check with your career center to find out what it has to offer and how you can gain access.

Informational Interviewing

After you have used print and electronic media to research careers, you'll benefit greatly from interviewing people who are already employed in occupations you're still considering. Informational interviewing may be the most direct and efficient source of career information of all.

Informational interviewing is not job interviewing. When you interview for a job, someone asks you questions. When you interview for information about a career, *you* ask the questions. See the box titled "Informational Interviewing: Questions to Ask About a Potential Career" for a list of questions you may want to ask during an informational interview.

Primary sources for informational interviews are people you already know. Think about whether anyone you know, or even a friend of a friend, works in a career you're considering. You can also use the telephone directory to contact persons who are working in careers you're exploring. Also, use the Internet to find local chapters of professional associations. Their Web sites usually have basic information about the field and contact information for the associations' leadership.

Be aware that some of the people you call may not even have 5 or 10 minutes to speak with you. Don't get discouraged. You'll probably be surprised at the number of people working in a career area who actually get excited about the opportunity to talk with someone interested in pursuing the same career that they've selected—especially if they particularly like or dislike their choice.

An important first step in this process is setting up the initial appointment. When you introduce yourself to potential interviewees, be sure to explain that you're in the process of exploring career options. Then tell them that you'd like to spend a few minutes talking with them about their career. You might want to let them know a little bit about your background and why you're considering a career in their field of expertise.

If possible, make an interview appointment at the individual's workplace. This is not only more convenient for the person you interview, but it also gives you an opportunity to witness firsthand the work environment of the career you're considering.

Informational Interviewing: Questions to Ask About a Potential Career

- What interested you in this career?
- What preparation did you need for obtaining this job?
- What do you like most about your career?
- What do you like least about your career?
- What are your job responsibilities?
- What kinds of stress do you experience on the job?
- What personal qualities are important in your line of work?
- What are the current prospects and job opportunities in this career?
- Is this career field expanding? In what ways is it changing?
- What is the salary range for persons in this career?
- What are the opportunities for promotion?
- If you were to give advice to someone considering this career, what would it be?
- Are there any sources of information about this career that you're aware of?
- Are there any Web sites you know of that relate to this career?

CASE STUDIES TO CONSIDER

Helen

Helen is an example of someone who discovered the value of informational interviewing as she explored various career options. Helen had been a homemaker for many years. Her youngest child was in fourth grade, and she wanted to return to the workforce. Helen's husband was very supportive of her decision to go back to work and encouraged her to meet with a career counselor to explore the possibilities. She was particularly interested in pursuing a career that directly involved helping others. It also was important for Helen to find a career that offered local employment opportunities. The last thing that she wanted to do was to uproot her family for the sole purpose of locating work.

After meeting with a career counselor for several weeks, Helen narrowed down her list of career options to nursing, teaching, and counseling. The information she gathered from traditional sources, such as the online version of the *OOH* and the *Guide to Occupational Exploration,* was somewhat helpful, but she was still having a difficult time figuring out which career would be best for her to pursue. Then, following the recommendation offered by her career counselor, Helen decided to interview nurses, teachers, and counselors.

By talking with nurses in the area, Helen discovered that there were many openings in nearly every nursing field. Helen was leaning toward psychiatric nursing, one of the specialties for which there was a particular need in her community. Her interviews with teachers and counselors, however, revealed the opposite to be true for those careers. Teachers mentioned how difficult it was to find a job in the local market, and counselors described difficulty in finding and maintaining a client base large enough to stay in business. This information was extremely valuable to Helen. As you might have guessed, Helen decided to become a registered nurse. Today she is the lead nurse at a large psychiatric hospital in Minnesota.

As you can see, informational interviews can be very helpful sources in career exploration. Don't forget to use this option when seeking information about the careers you're considering.

Community Leaders

Another way to get information about job trends in your city, county, or region is to contact some of the leaders in your community. Chambers of commerce and other business organizations and clubs can offer helpful information as well as networking opportunities. Getting to know business and community leaders can also prove essential to securing employment. Try to make some of these valuable contacts as you continue the career exploration process.

Friends and Family

Friends and family members can be sources of helpful information about careers. As you begin narrowing down your career options, don't forget to get feedback from those who know you best.

National Career Development Association

The National Career Development Association (NCDA) is an organization of career counseling professionals. Each year the NCDA compiles a listing of current career literature that you may find helpful as you explore various career options. The list is published each summer in the association's journal, *The Career Development Quarterly*. Information about the journal and other publications sponsored by the NCDA is available online at http://www.ncda.org.

Local Trade Associations and Unions

Another way to gather accurate information about various occupations is to contact local trade associations and unions. They'll be glad to provide you with information about local job trends, working conditions, and projected employment opportunities. You'll find contact information for trade associations and unions in the phone book.

CASE STUDIES TO CONSIDER

Emma

Emma was interested in a career as a heating and air conditioning repairperson. She obtained some general information about the career using the online *OOH* and by reading several articles in recent newspapers and magazines at her library. But the information that was the most helpful was provided by the local heating, ventilation, and air conditioning (HVAC) union. Union representatives sent Emma a brochure that explained the process of becoming an HVAC apprentice, something that is required to become a member of the union. After meeting with the president of the local union, Emma obtained an apprenticeship assignment with one of the workers in town. She completed her training and apprenticeship program and is now the vice president of the local HVAC union.

Completing Exercise 7.1, "Using the Career Information Form," for each of the careers you're considering at this time will help you summarize the information you gather about those careers from the resources described in this chapter.

EXERCISE 7.1   *USING THE CAREER INFORMATION FORM*

Two blank Career Information Forms appear at the end of the chapter. Feel free to make additional copies so that you can complete this exercise for each of the careers you're exploring.

In the space provided at the top of each form, write in the careers that you'd like to learn more about. You will probably want to look back at the short list you generated at the end of Chapter 6. Using the various sources of information discussed in this chapter, try to answer as many of the questions about each career as possible.

Don't get discouraged if it takes a few days or weeks to complete this project. You may have to consult several sources before finding out all of the information for each career you're considering. The career decisions you'll be making are going to directly influence many aspects of your life. Devoting a substantial amount of time and energy to this process is well worth the investment!

The sample below will give you an idea of how you might go about completing these forms. The information to complete the sample form was obtained from several sources, including O*NET, the online *OOH,* a few newspaper articles, informational interviews with computer programmers, and DISCOVER (one of the computerized career information and guidance systems mentioned earlier).

A Sample Career Information Form

GENERAL INFORMATION

Title of Career: Computer Programmer

NATURE OF WORK

General Working Conditions: Computer programmers usually work in offices that are relatively comfortable and quiet. Some programmers work long hours or on weekends to meet deadlines. Many programmers are beginning to work out of their homes as they engage in telecommuting or consulting work.

Employee Responsibilities: Computer programmers write specific programs by breaking down each step into a logical series of instructions the computer can follow. They then code these instructions in a conventional programming language, such as COBOL; an artificial intelligence language such as Prolog; or a more advanced language, such as Java, C++, or Visual Basic. Many programmers also are involved in updating, repairing, modifying, and expanding existing programs.

Physical Demands: Sometimes long hours of sedentary work are required, often at a desk or in an office.

Potential Work Hazards: Computer programmers are susceptible to eyestrain, back discomfort, and hand and wrist problems, such as carpal tunnel syndrome.

EMPLOYMENT TRENDS AND PROJECTIONS

Current Supply and Demand for Workers: About 455,000 computer programmers were working in 2004 in a variety of industries. There were also approximately 25,000 self-employed computer programmers in 2004. Many programmers work for engineering and management services companies, telecommunications companies, manufacturers of computer equipment, and government agencies.

Future Prospects: Employment of programmers is expected to grow more slowly than average as sophisticated software programs are now capable of writing the basic code once done by entry-level programmers. In addition, many of these jobs are being outsourced to other countries.

Stability of Employment: Because of the need for companies and organizations to keep up with constantly updated technologies, most computer programmers—once hired—are able to remain relatively stable in their work roles.

Opportunities for Advancement: There are many opportunities for computer programmers to advance into managerial or higher-paying programming positions over time. Advanced positions in computer programming may include lead programmer, programming analyst, and research and development manager. Many programmers elect to begin small companies or businesses or to serve in a consultation role.

QUALIFICATIONS

General Qualifications for Employment: Required skills vary from job to job, but most programmers are expected to be proficient in a number of programming languages, especially the newer, object-oriented languages, such as C++, Visual Basic, and Java.

Educational/Training Requirements: Because of the growing number of qualified applicants and the increasing complexity of many programming tasks, bachelor's degrees are commonly required, although some programmers can still find good jobs with a two-year degree or certificate. Still, it's probably the case that most employers will hire someone with lots of experience even if the person lacks a particular degree or formal training credential. Recent college graduates can usually improve their employment prospects by participating in a college work-study program or by completing an internship.

Minimum Aptitude: Again, this varies from company to company, but employers tend to look for candidates who possess the necessary programming skills *and* who can think logically and pay close attention to details. Computer programming jobs tend to require patience, persistence, and the ability to work on exacting analytical work, especially under pressure.

Preparation Standards: Completion of *at least* a two-year certificate or degree program is necessary; a bachelor's degree is probably a better idea. Some internship or cooperative learning experience would probably be a good idea, too. Learning several programming languages will increase employment opportunities. Professional certification also may provide a job seeker in this field a competitive advantage.

WORKLOAD AND SALARY INFORMATION

Typical Hours Worked Each Week/Month: Although most programmers average between 40 and 50 hours of work a week, their hours are sometimes flexible (depending on the company they work for). Most programmers are on salary and are not hourly employees. As a result, they do not necessarily get compensated for overtime work.

Salary Range: Median annual earnings of computer programmers in 2004 were $62,890, with the middle 50 percent of programmers earning between $47,580 and $81,280. Starting salary offers for graduates with a bachelor's degree in computer programming averaged $50,820 a year in 2005.

Benefits: Besides the usual health, dental, vision, and retirement benefits, which vary from company to company, most computer programmers have the luxury of working on some of the most powerful and advanced computers available.

RELATED OCCUPATIONS

Computer scientist, computer engineer, systems analyst, operations research analyst, database administrator.

SOURCES OF ADDITIONAL INFORMATION

Association for Computing Machinery, 1515 Broadway, New York, NY 10036. Internet: http://www.acm.org.

Institute of Electrical and Electronics Engineers Computer Society, Headquarters Office, 1730 Massachusetts Ave. NW, Washington, DC 20036-1992. Internet: http://www.computer.org.

National Workforce Center for Emerging Technologies, 3000 Landerholm Circle SE, Bellevue, WA 98007. Internet: http://www.nwcet.org.

By collecting facts, figures, and impressions of different careers, you can compare the nuts and bolts of what each career entails. At the same time, there are nuances that you also want to consider. It is much like the difference between buying clothes online and going to a department store and trying them on. Both provide you with clothes, but one provides a much more personalized check for fit.

JOB SHADOWING

In addition to gathering the information to complete the Career Information Forms, another effective method to help you narrow down your career options is **job shadowing.** Job shadowing refers to a hands-on exercise in which you learn about many of the day-to-day tasks and responsibilities associated with careers you're considering. When you job shadow, you follow workers around (as if you were their shadow) as they engage in the duties associated with their jobs.

The benefits of job shadowing are numerous. Not only will you be able to get a firsthand sense of what employment in particular careers is really all about, but you might also have the opportunity to make some important job contacts that could come in handy in the future.

CASE STUDIES TO CONSIDER

Karina

In addition to career counseling, mentoring programs can help people discover more about themselves and the world of work. In one such program, college students were connected with alumni in their vocational area of choice. Students interested in finding a mentor were required to fill out an application and meet with a career counselor. One student, Karina, wanted to be a forensic scientist. She loved watching forensic dramas on television and liked the idea of using her interest in chemistry and problem-solving skills to solve crimes. She was matched with a scientist who fit well with Karina's aspirations. They talked on the phone and met for coffee and finally arranged to have Karina spend the week of spring break shadowing the scientists in the lab. When Karina went to see her career counselor later that semester to talk about her experiences, she said that the program was phenomenal and had changed her life. When the counselor expressed excitement that the experience had been so positive, Karina quickly corrected her and told her it had been awful! Although all of the scientists she met loved their careers, Karina experienced the week as tedious, boring, and far too focused on paperwork. While she enjoyed the science, she realized that she did not want to practice it in such detail each and every day. Karina was thrilled to discover the lack of fit before she invested years in pursuing a career she would not have liked. Karina shadowed three other professionals before deciding to study criminal justice.

Exercise 7.2, "Job Shadowing," will help you prepare for and evaluate your job shadowing experiences.

A. First, decide which careers you'd like to job shadow. Based on the results of the previous exercise, you may have already started narrowing down your list of preferred careers. Consider job shadowing each career you're still exploring.

List below those careers that you'd like to job shadow:

1. _____
2. _____
3. _____
4. _____
5. _____

B. The next step is to contact individuals who are working in the careers you've listed. Many of the resources described in this chapter can provide you with helpful information in this regard. You'll probably have the best results in locating someone to shadow by using the telephone directory, contacting community leaders, checking with trade organizations and associations, and asking friends and family members for contacts. Local offices of the state employment service and your college's career center may also be able to help you.

Try to get in touch with the company's human resources director if you don't already know an employee you can observe on the job. The human resources director will probably be able to provide you with general information regarding job shadowing at that company, as well as put you in contact with particular employees you might be able to shadow. Don't assume that the person you talk with will know what job shadowing is all about. Explain that you're in the process of making some career decisions and that you'd like to observe the work that goes on in their setting for a few hours.

It might be a good idea to job shadow the same career more than once, with employees from different companies or organizations. You probably won't be making any definitive conclusions about a career based solely on job shadowing. Still, with only one shadowing experience for a particular career option, you risk getting a biased view of that career.

C. You'll have the opportunity during the job-shadowing exercise to observe a variety of things about the nature of a particular career. Pay especially close attention to those details that are likely to influence your decision of whether or not to continue pursuing a career in that particular industry. Take a look at the Job Shadow Evaluation Form before engaging in your first shadowing experience to get an idea of some of the important questions you should be thinking about during the exercise.

D. Make as many copies of the Job Shadow Evaluation Form as you need. After each of your job-shadowing experiences, use the form to evaluate your experience. As you complete the forms, focus on information you learned about the career that you weren't aware of prior to job shadowing.

Job Shadow Evaluation Form

Title of Career: _____

Job Shadow Date and Time: _____

Business Name: _____

Address: _____

Contact Person: _____   Phone: _____

Job Title: _____

GENERAL WORKING CONDITIONS:

_____

_____

_____

_____

_____

TASKS AND DUTIES:

_____

_____

_____

_____

_____

THINGS I LEARNED ABOUT THAT I DIDN'T ALREADY KNOW:

_____

_____

_____

_____

_____

OVERALL IMPRESSIONS OF THE JOB:

_____

_____

_____

_____

_____

THE VALUE OF PART-TIME AND VOLUNTEER EXPERIENCES

Perhaps the most comprehensive method for gathering information about potential careers is to obtain actual part-time or volunteer work experience. One of the best ways to learn about a career is to obtain on-the-job experience. Although it may not always be easy to identify part-time or volunteer work that's available in the career fields you're interested in, you may be surprised by how many opportunities actually exist for you to obtain such experience.

If obtaining part-time work in careers you're considering isn't easy, then you might try getting some experience in a field that's related to your career interests. Someone who's considering a career as a financial planner, for example, may not

One of the best ways to learn about a career is to obtain on-the-job experience.

find any jobs or volunteer experiences in financial planning per se, but there may be other part-time opportunities available related to financial planning. Work as a bank teller or tax assistant might at least let you see what occupations related to financial management are all about.

Working part-time or volunteering in a career you're exploring will allow you to see if it's the right career for you.

Many academic departments at colleges and universities have established relationships with companies and organizations within the community that offer part-time work or volunteer opportunities. Career centers on most campuses offer a variety of internship and cooperative learning activities that may be able to provide you with similar experiences. Connections you may have through a religious or community service organization might also help you identify potential sites for obtaining volunteer work experience. Appendix D provides a brief overview of several job search strategies that you might find helpful as you search for part-time or volunteer job openings.

QUESTIONS FOR CRITICAL THOUGHT

1. Which of the resources described in this chapter do you think will be most useful to you as you gather important information about careers you're considering? Why do you think these particular resources will be most helpful?
2. How can accessing the online version of the OOH help you make effective career decisions?
3. What are some of the benefits that come from engaging in job shadowing as a method of career exploration?
4. How might you go about searching for a part-time job or volunteer experience in a career that you're currently considering?

KEY CONCEPTS TO REMEMBER

- Create a file for each of the occupations included in your "short list" of career possibilities.
- Job shadowing can teach you about many of the day-to-day tasks and responsibilities associated with the careers you're considering.
- Part-time or volunteer work is a useful method of gathering information about potential careers.

Career Information Form

Title of Career: _____

NATURE OF WORK

General Working Conditions:

_____
_____
_____
_____
_____

Employee Responsibilities:

_____
_____
_____
_____
_____

Physical Demands:

_____
_____
_____
_____
_____

Potential Work Hazards:

_____
_____
_____
_____
_____

EMPLOYMENT TRENDS AND PROJECTIONS

Current Supply and Demand for Workers:

_____
_____
_____
_____
_____

Future Prospects:

_____

_____

_____

_____

Stability of Employment:

_____

_____

_____

_____

Opportunities for Advancement:

_____

_____

_____

_____

QUALIFICATIONS

General Qualifications for Employment:

_____

_____

_____

_____

Educational/Training Requirements:

_____

_____

_____

_____

Minimum Aptitude:

_____

_____

_____

_____

Preparation Standards:

_____

_____

_____

_____

WORKLOAD AND SALARY INFORMATION

Typical Hours Worked Each Week/Month:

_____

_____

_____

_____

Salary Range:

_____

_____

_____

_____

Benefits:

_____

_____

_____

_____

RELATED OCCUPATIONS

_____

_____

_____

_____

_____

_____

SOURCES OF ADDITIONAL INFORMATION

_____

_____

_____

_____

_____

_____

Career Information Form

Title of Career: _____

NATURE OF WORK

General Working Conditions:

_____
_____
_____
_____

Employee Responsibilities:

_____
_____
_____
_____
_____

Physical Demands:

_____
_____
_____
_____

Potential Work Hazards:

_____
_____
_____
_____

EMPLOYMENT TRENDS AND PROJECTIONS

Current Supply and Demand for Workers:

_____

Future Prospects:

_____
_____
_____
_____

Stability of Employment:

_____

_____

_____

_____

Opportunities for Advancement:

_____

_____

_____

_____

QUALIFICATIONS

General Qualifications for Employment:

_____

_____

_____

_____

Educational/Training Requirements:

_____

_____

_____

_____

Minimum Aptitude:

_____

_____

_____

_____

Preparation Standards:

_____

_____

_____

_____

WORKLOAD AND SALARY INFORMATION

Typical Hours Worked Each Week/Month:

_____

_____

_____

Salary Range:

_____

_____

_____

Benefits:

_____

_____

_____

RELATED OCCUPATIONS

_____

_____

_____

_____

_____

_____

SOURCES OF ADDITIONAL INFORMATION

_____

_____

_____

_____

_____

Meeting the Challenges Head-On

IDENTIFYING AND OVERCOMING BARRIERS

As you narrow down your career options, it will be increasingly important for you to consider your chances of achieving your various career goals. One of the best ways to engage in that process is to consider potential hurdles that may interfere with your career development and then to develop strategies to overcome them.

The primary purpose of this chapter is to introduce you to the types of hurdles or barriers that could interfere with your chances of success. You'll learn about the differences between internal and external barriers as well as real versus perceived barriers. You will read several case studies to gain a clearer understanding of the roles that barriers play in the career decision-making process. You'll also have the opportunity to learn about effective strategies for overcoming those barriers.

BARRIERS IN CAREER EXPLORATION

Career counselors have long recognized the role that barriers play in the career decision-making process. Barriers are those obstacles that may deter you from reaching a particular career goal. Whether the information we have about particular barriers is accurate or not, we often compromise our career goals based on the barriers we perceive. If we *believe* that a certain career is not possible because of certain barriers, we might compromise our goals and consider alternative career options instead. But recognizing the barriers to achieving our career goals doesn't have to result in compromise. The more we're aware of potential barriers, the more likely we are to be prepared when we actually face them. This process begins with an understanding of the different types of barriers that can occur throughout the career decision-making process.

The more we're aware of potential barriers, the more likely we are to be prepared when we actually face them.

Many of the barriers that influence our career decisions are *internal* barriers. These barriers come from inside of us. We usually have a fair amount of control over internal barriers and, through hard work and effort, can often overcome them. A lack of confidence in your ability to complete a degree, procrastination, poor study habits, the fear of failure, and concerns about juggling multiple life roles are a few examples of internal barriers.

Other kinds of career-related barriers are *external* barriers. These barriers come from sources outside of us. We usually have little, if any, control over these barriers. Global economic trends, educational requirements associated with a particular career, discrimination, and employment projections are examples of external barriers. Although we have a more difficult time controlling external barriers, identifying them can help us achieve our career goals.

Some common examples of internal and external barriers are listed in the box titled "Examples of Internal and External Barriers." Although this listing is certainly not all encompassing, it does give you an idea of the differences between internal and external barriers, a distinction that may help as you consider the barriers associated with your career possibilities.

The important thing to remember is that countless resources exist to help you overcome barriers, and—in the long run—the ability to demonstrate that you have overcome obstacles can be a very marketable trait.

Many people consider various aspects of their background to be potential barriers to career development. Sometimes a person will view her or his racial background, gender, sexual orientation, religious beliefs, socioeconomic status, or physical disability as a barrier to career success. These factors can be especially problematic if you expect them to lead to discrimination and prejudice on the job. The important thing to remember is that countless resources exist to help you overcome these and other related barriers, and—in the long run—the ability to demonstrate that you have overcome obstacles can be a very marketable trait.

Examples of Internal and External Barriers

INTERNAL BARRIERS

- Anxiety associated with making career decisions
- Concerns about multiple life roles and responsibilities
- Low confidence in your ability to obtain a particular degree
- Poor study habits
- Procrastination

EXTERNAL BARRIERS

- Economic trends
- Educational requirements
- Employment outlook
- Lack of local educational/training opportunities
- Lack of funds to pursue a career

DISCRIMINATION

Discrimination is a particularly tricky barrier in that it can be both internal and external. In other words, discrimination can be an obstacle if someone decides not to hire or promote you because of some aspect of who are you or if you decide to avoid a career because you fear that discrimination will be an obstacle you won't be able to overcome.

In terms of employment discrimination on the basis of age, gender, racial and ethnic background, religious beliefs, sexual orientation, and disability status, you need to remember that discrimination in *any* form is illegal. Employers are required to hire people on the basis of their qualifications, not their age, gender, race, religion, sexual orientation, or disability status. The reality is, however, that not all discrimination is overt and you may not know that it's happening. If you are aware of illegal discrimination, such as being asked illegal questions during an interview, how you will address that discrimination is entirely up to you. For example, if someone asks you an illegal (or even inappropriate) question in a job interview, you have three choices. First, you can simply answer the question. Although it is illegal to ask for information that is not related to the job, answering the question is not. Remember that you have no idea where the interviewer's biases come from. As such, you may not know how the information will be used. But if you're comfortable with the question and your answer, that is fine. Second, you can refuse to answer the question, which is well within your rights. You should phrase your refusal carefully and try not to come across as uncooperative or confrontational, as most employers are not looking for those traits in employees. Third, you can think about the real intent of the question and try to answer the "real" question being asked. For example, if an interviewer asked if you have children, you can respond that there is nothing in your personal life that will interfere with your ability to travel or be at work on time. Obviously, this is a tricky issue in that you want to make a good impression while being sure to protect your rights. Being open and honest about your concerns is usually the best way to go. If you have any doubt regarding your treatment in an employment setting, contact the Equal Employment Opportunity/Affirmative Action office in your community.

Persons with disabilities, both physical and mental, often wonder how they'll be able to engage in certain kinds of work. Knowledge about available resources is a key factor to overcoming these potential barriers. The Americans with Disabilities Act (ADA), passed in 1990, protects all individuals from job discrimination on the basis of disabilities (which covers all physiological conditions affecting one or more of the body's systems as well as mental and psychological disorders). Visual, hearing, and speech impairments, cerebral palsy, epilepsy, muscular dystrophy, multiple sclerosis, HIV, cancer, diabetes, emotional illness, and learning disabilities are just a few of the types of disabilities protected under the law.

In her book *Job Strategies for People with Disabilities*, Melanie Witt explains that prospective employers must provide "reasonable accommodations" to employees who have a disability of some sort. These accommodations can range from making a building more accessible to offering variable work hours to employees with special needs. Special equipment might be purchased or changes in the work environment might be made to help employees complete their tasks more efficiently.

Most college and universities have someone who is responsible for assisting students with disabilities in all aspects of their educational and career development. The Dean of Students Office would be able to direct you to the appropriate resources on your campus. To find out more about the services available to persons with disabilities in your state, contact the state government office responsible for ensuring compliance with ADA regulations.

In addition, the Office of Disability Employment Policy of the U.S. Department of Labor offers a fabulous resource called the Job Accommodation Network, or JAN.

This free service consults with individuals and organizations to provide appropriate accommodation solutions, provides technical assistance on related legal issues, and provides assistance for individuals who are or would like to be self-employed. Its Web site, http://www.jan.wvu.edu/, provides all kinds of resources for individuals with disabilities as well as contact information. In addition, the office offers a toll-free helpline at 800-526-7234 or 877-781-9403 (TTY).

REAL AND PERCEIVED BARRIERS

As you begin to think about the kinds of barriers that are relevant to your life situation, you'll also want to distinguish between *real* and *perceived* barriers.

CASE STUDIES TO CONSIDER

Gloria

Gloria decided that she was going to go back to school to pursue a degree in criminal justice. Gloria was in her late forties, and her two children were grown and living on their own. Gloria had always thought about returning to school to become qualified to work in law enforcement. With more free time on her hands, Gloria decided to begin to make that dream a reality.

Like many people who return to the world of work after several years away, Gloria was starting to wonder if she really had what it takes to succeed in an academic training program. She had made a list of obstacles that she believed were likely to interfere with her career goal.

One of the barriers Gloria had listed was weak writing skills. When Gloria's career counselor, who also worked as an academic advisor at the community college, asked her how she had reached that conclusion, Gloria mentioned that it had been almost 25 years since she had written a formal paper in school. When her career counselor asked whether she had received any recent feedback about her writing skills, Gloria began to realize that her perception wasn't based on actual feedback, but rather on her hunch that she *probably* had poor written communication skills relative to other college students.

As Gloria continued working with her career counselor, it became increasingly apparent that many of the barriers she had listed were not really as problematic as she had thought. Her results on the college placement tests, for example, revealed that Gloria's writing skills were actually above average for college students. The increased awareness that came from Gloria's identification and consideration of perceived barriers, along with the results of actual skills assessments, proved to be very useful in helping Gloria make more informed career decisions.

Not only did Gloria succeed in her writing classes at college, she actually became a journalist, obtaining a position at the local newspaper upon graduation!

In Chapter 9 you'll be narrowing down your list of career options even further than you have already. But before you make those decisions, think about the potential barriers that might develop as you continue to engage in the career exploration process. After developing a list of potential career-related barriers, you'll be able to work on identifying specific methods for overcoming those barriers.

Identifying barriers is easier for some people than it is for others. Many people are already aware of the barriers that stand in their way of reaching the goals they've set for themselves. Others need some help identifying them. Furthermore, many barriers—both internal and external—can seem like insurmountable obstacles. But identifying specific barriers associated with careers can help you determine what steps you need to take in order to overcome those hurdles.

CASE STUDIES TO CONSIDER

Juan

Juan was a high school senior who was very interested in becoming a professional athlete. His parents were concerned that by focusing on a career in professional sports, Juan was ignoring other careers that he might be more likely to succeed in. Juan was a first-generation college student. In fact, he was the only one in his family ever to graduate from high school. His parents, both of whom came from a low socioeconomic background, wanted to do all that they could to ensure Juan's success.

When Juan outlined his career goals, he explained to his career counselor that he was really only interested in pursuing a career as a professional baseball player. When his counselor asked Juan to explain reasons for his interest in professional sports, it became apparent that he enjoyed the outdoors, found satisfaction in a competitive environment, and liked the possibility of earning (as he put it) "a whole lot of money." Besides, he was one of the best baseball players in his state.

Juan's counselor asked him to outline some of the barriers that might interfere with his career goal. His initial response was that there really weren't any barriers, no reason at all to think that he wouldn't succeed as a professional baseball player. The way he looked at it, because he had received numerous awards in high school because of his excellent performance, he had no reason to think that succeeding in professional sports would be any different. Juan's counselor's purpose in working with him wasn't to persuade him to change his mind about a career as a professional player, nor did his counselor want to decrease Juan's confidence in his abilities. The counselor simply wanted him to recognize that there might be some barriers to becoming a professional baseball player—just as there are for any career option.

Juan's counselor encouraged him to talk with some of his friends and family members. His counselor also arranged for Juan to interview three professional athletes about some of the barriers that they had experienced over the years. After Juan conducted the informational interviews, he developed a list of potential barriers based on what he had learned. As his counselor had hoped, Juan was eventually able to cite several barriers, both external and internal, that he hadn't considered before.

Juan still decided to pursue a career as a professional athlete and enjoyed his life as a professional baseball player for over 10 years! After considering all of the potential barriers to becoming a professional athlete and establishing ways to overcome them, Juan was able to proceed with his career goal with increased knowledge and confidence. When he encountered inevitable obstacles, he was not surprised and had developed strategies and resources for addressing them that helped in his long-term career success.

The experiences of Gloria and Juan illustrate why identifying potential barriers to career goals is so important. By evaluating perceived barriers, Gloria obtained a more realistic appraisal of her skills. By identifying possible barriers related to becoming a professional athlete, Juan was better able to prepare to meet the challenges he encountered along the way.

Exercise 8.1 is designed to help you generate a list of potential barriers associated with the career options you're considering. It's important to consider all barriers, internal *and* external, associated with each of your career options. Exercises 8.2 and 8.3 will help you develop strategies for overcoming those barriers as you begin clearing the way for the final stages of the career exploration and planning process.

EXERCISE 8.1   *IDENTIFYING CAREER-RELATED BARRIERS*

We're best able to identify potential barriers to a particular career goal when we draw on many sources of information. Of course, you're the best person to determine which barriers are most applicable to your particular situation. But talking with friends, family members, and other persons may help you identify a few barriers that you might not otherwise come up with.

All of the information (including your research, information interviews, job shadowing, and work experience) that you've gathered up to this point about the world of work will probably help you identify many of the internal and external barriers associated with careers you're considering. Consult that information, and talk with the people who know you best as you develop your lists of barriers for each career option.

CAREER OPTION:

INTERNAL BARRIERS:

_____

_____

_____

_____

EXTERNAL BARRIERS:

_____

_____

_____

_____

CAREER OPTION:

INTERNAL BARRIERS:

_____

_____

_____

_____

EXTERNAL BARRIERS:

_____

_____

_____

_____

CAREER OPTION:

INTERNAL BARRIERS:

_____

_____

_____

_____

EXTERNAL BARRIERS:

_____

_____

_____

_____

CAREER OPTION:

INTERNAL BARRIERS:

_____

_____

_____

_____

EXTERNAL BARRIERS:

_____

_____

_____

_____

CAREER OPTION:

INTERNAL BARRIERS:

_____

_____

_____

_____

EXTERNAL BARRIERS:

_____

_____

_____

_____

CAREER OPTION:

INTERNAL BARRIERS:

_____

_____

_____

_____

EXTERNAL BARRIERS:

_____

_____

_____

_____

You'll refer to these lists of barriers later in the chapter as you begin to develop strategies for overcoming and/or coping with them.

CAREER SELF-EFFICACY

The contributions of Dr. Albert Bandura, one of the world's most renowned psychologists, have helped us gain important insights into human behavior. One of Bandura's contributions that has been especially helpful in the area of career counseling is the concept of self-efficacy.

Self-efficacy is an individual's confidence in his or her ability to accomplish a specific task. For example, if a 300-pound barbell were on the floor in front of you, and someone asked you how confident you were in your ability to dead-lift the barbell on a scale of one (no confidence at all) to five (very high confidence), you might respond by saying "one." Your confidence level might be relatively low when it comes to lifting large amounts of weight. If that were the case, Bandura would say that you have low self-efficacy for lifting the 300-pound barbell. Your particular level of self-efficacy for lifting a 300-pound barbell is influenced by several factors, which we will discuss shortly.

This concept of self-efficacy directly applies to overcoming career-related barriers. For instance, if you're not very confident in your ability to overcome certain barriers, it would be appropriate to say that you have low self-efficacy for overcoming those barriers. If, on the other hand, you believe that you can overcome many potential career barriers without much of a problem, it would be appropriate to say you have high self-efficacy.

One of the most interesting things that Bandura and other researchers found about self-efficacy is that the likelihood of completing a particular task is directly linked with your level of self-efficacy associated with that task. To put it another way, if you're confident in your ability to accomplish something, then odds are that you'll accomplish it. If, on the other hand, you aren't very confident in your ability to complete a task, then odds are that you'll fail at it. As the ancient Roman poet Virgil noted, "They can because they think they can."

Identifying barriers for certain career options is only the beginning of the process. Once you've identified particular barriers related to the careers you're exploring, you need to work on increasing your confidence (or self-efficacy) and your skills for overcoming those barriers. Granted, there may be many barriers (especially external barriers) that simply cannot be overcome. There isn't a whole lot you can do, for example, to overcome problems with the global economy. But there may be lots you can do to overcome many of the internal barriers you listed in Exercise 8.1 or strategies you can develop for coping with obstacles you can't entirely overcome.

Increasing your confidence in your ability to accomplish your career goals can play an important role in career decision making.

Once you've identified particular barriers related to the careers you're exploring, you need to work on increasing your self-confidence (or self-efficacy) and your skills for overcoming those barriers.

CASE STUDIES TO CONSIDER

Anna

Consider the case of Anna. Anna was an 18-year-old, first-year community college student. She had been diagnosed with multiple sclerosis at the end of her senior year of high school. Schoolwork had always been a challenge for Anna, and academic work in college was no exception. Her physical condition was becoming especially challenging, and Anna was beginning to think that obtaining a college degree might not be possible after all.

Instead of giving up, however, Anna contacted the Dean of Students Office to find out if there were any services on campus that she could use. She discovered that there was an Office of Special Student Services that could assist with her educational and career concerns. After meeting with the director of Special Student Services, Anna realized that *many* support services were available to empower her to succeed. Her confidence or self-efficacy for obtaining a college degree increased dramatically because she took the time to explore sources of support available right on campus.

Four years later, Anna proudly graduated and entered a prestigious medical school. She eventually became an obstetrician/gynecologist and currently works in a group practice in New Mexico.

This is especially true when it comes to your confidence or self-efficacy for overcoming career-related barriers. Let's take a closer look at Bandura's concept of self-efficacy.

Bandura explained that four factors contribute to our level of self-efficacy for a particular task.

- *Previous Experiences* (or Performance Accomplishments)
  Past experiences we've had performing the task.

- *Vicarious Learning*
  Learning about our own abilities to accomplish a task by watching others.

- *Verbal Persuasion*
  The degree to which other people around us persuade or encourage us to accomplish a task.

- *Physiological Arousal*
  How excited or anxious we get as we try to accomplish a task.

To get a better idea of how these factors influence our self-efficacy, let's return to the 300-pound barbell example. In terms of your *previous experiences*, suppose you have *never* been able to dead-lift any more than 180 pounds (and that much only on a *very* good day). Because of your experiences, you would be fairly sure that you lack the ability to lift a 300-pound barbell. If, on the other hand, you were able to lift 300 pounds in the past, or at least some amount of weight closer to it (say 275 or 280 pounds), odds are that your self-efficacy for lifting 300 pounds would be much higher.

In terms of *vicarious learning*, the second source of self-efficacy, perhaps—like many of us—you've learned from watching others that it is very difficult to lift 300 pounds. To put it in self-efficacy terms, you've learned vicariously (from watching other people) that you're not likely to lift 300 pounds.

In terms of *verbal persuasion*, you probably haven't had too many people strongly *encouraging* you to lift 300 pounds. It's no surprise that your self-efficacy for lifting 300 pounds would be so low. Verbal persuasion influences our self-efficacy for accomplishing a task by either encouraging or discouraging us from trying to accomplish it.

The fourth factor that influences our self-efficacy is *physiological arousal*. Psychologists discovered long ago that we tend to perform best when we experience only a moderate degree of anxiety or arousal associated with performing a task. Of course, too much anxiety or arousal can be even more detrimental than no anxiety at all. The lesson here is that a little arousal is not a bad thing. What Bandura and his colleagues discovered, as you might expect, is that our self-efficacy for accomplishing a given task is related to the amount of anxiety we experience when engaging in that task.

There's quite a lot we can do to influence the sources of self-efficacy for any specific task. For instance, consider the role that previous experience plays in the development of our self-efficacy. If we have low self-efficacy for overcoming a particular barrier, then we might need to seek new experiences that will allow us the opportunity to try out different ways to overcome that barrier.

Take, for example, a person's low self-efficacy for lifting a 300-pound barbell. One way that a person might be able to increase her or his self-efficacy for lifting that much weight would be to identify new experiences that might increase her or his chances of lifting it in the future. If you were to set up some short-term goals, perhaps increasing your weight-lifting ability to dead-lift 200 pounds by the end of this month, 225 pounds by the end of next month, and 275 pounds the month after that, you just might increase your chances for eventually lifting 300 pounds.

This same process can work for overcoming career-related barriers.

CASE STUDIES TO CONSIDER

Nelle

Nelle was a young woman who sought counseling at her college career center. She had been studying music most of her life and came to the university as a music major. Nelle had received a great deal of praise and attention for her piano and singing skills in high school, but she was overwhelmed by the level of skill of her fellow college students.

She was also struggling with the advanced theoretical courses required of her major. By the time she went to counseling, she was looking for a new major that would be easier for her.

Before leaping into a new exploration, her counselor asked how confident she was in her decision to leave music. It quickly became apparent that she still loved the major, but she was not sure she could be successful. The counselor asked her whether she would stay in music if she had more confidence in her abilities, and she said she would. She was encouraged to speak with other students further along in the program to ask if they had ever had doubts about their skills (vicarious learning). Then she was encouraged to ask her faculty advisor for an honest assessment of her potential within the major (verbal persuasion). The counselor also introduced her to techniques for managing performance anxiety such as relaxed breathing (physiological arousal). Finally, she researched venues in the area that would provide her the opportunity to perform in front of different audiences (performance accomplishments). Nelle decided to delay her decision to change majors for another year. She eventually decided to stay a music major and in the summer of her junior year took a summer performance internship in New York.

You may find that you're fairly confident in your ability to overcome most of the barriers you listed in Exercise 8.1. If so, you're well on your way to benefiting from the process of identifying career-related barriers. However, if your self-efficacy for overcoming some of those barriers is less than perfect, Exercise 8.2 may be especially helpful.

SELF-EFFICACY CHANGE STRATEGIES	**EXERCISE 8.2**

Part I.

Go back to Exercise 8.1 and rate your self-efficacy for overcoming the barriers you listed for each career option. Rate your confidence, or self-efficacy level, for each identified barrier on a scale of 1 *(no confidence at all)* to 5 *(complete confidence)*. Write that number in the left margin next to each barrier that you listed. The rating scale shown below can serve as a guide.

1	2	3	4	5
no confidence	*very little confidence*	*some confidence*	*a lot of confidence*	*complete confidence*

Part II.

If your self-efficacy for overcoming a particular barrier is high (4 or 5), then you've probably already identified ways you might overcome that barrier. But if your confidence rating is low, you might want to identify some ways to increase your self-efficacy for overcoming that barrier.

Step 1. Look again at the lists of barriers in Exercise 8.1 and select three barriers for which your self-efficacy rating is 2 or lower. Write these barriers in the spaces provided on the Overcoming Identified Barriers section that follows.

Step 2. Think about each barrier you've listed and identify *new experiences* that you might seek in order to help you overcome the barrier.

Step 3. List ways that you can use *vicarious learning* to increase your self-efficacy for overcoming each barrier. Remember that vicarious learning involves discovering ways to overcome barriers by watching and learning from others. For example, you could find a role model or mentor who has overcome obstacles you would like to overcome.

Step 4. List ways that you can use *verbal persuasion* to increase your self-efficacy for overcoming each barrier. Verbal persuasion techniques that may help you overcome specific barriers might include asking your friends and family members to support you in your efforts, seeking the assistance of a counselor or academic advisor for on-going support, or finding a group to join of people seeking similar support.

Step 5. Finally, think about strategies you might use to increase your excitement and decrease your anxiety associated with each barrier. Strategies you might consider include stress reduction techniques, relaxation exercises, or some other method you've discovered in the past for effectively decreasing anxiety.

Overcoming Identified Barriers

POTENTIAL BARRIER:

WAYS TO INCREASE YOUR SELF-EFFICACY FOR OVERCOMING THE BARRIER:

New Experiences

_____

_____

_____

Vicarious Learning

_____

_____

_____

Verbal Persuasion

_____

_____

_____

Anxiety Reduction

_____

_____

_____

POTENTIAL BARRIER:

WAYS TO INCREASE YOUR SELF-EFFICACY FOR OVERCOMING THE BARRIER:

New Experiences

_____

_____

_____

Vicarious Learning

_____

_____

_____

Verbal Persuasion

_____

_____

_____

Anxiety Reduction

_____

_____

_____

POTENTIAL BARRIER:

WAYS TO INCREASE YOUR SELF-EFFICACY FOR OVERCOMING THE BARRIER:

New Experiences

_____

_____

_____

Vicarious Learning

_____

_____

_____

Verbal Persuasion

_____

_____

_____

Anxiety Reduction

_____

_____

_____

Whether or not you'll overcome career-related barriers ultimately depends on how much time and energy you devote to increasing your self-efficacy for overcoming them. We'll spend some additional time in Chapter 9 identifying other action strategies that will be useful in the pursuit of your career goals.

IDENTIFYING HELPFUL RESOURCES

As previously mentioned, friends and family members can be important sources of encouragement and support, not only as you work on identifying and overcoming career-related barriers but also throughout the career decision-making process. The social network that your friends and family members provide is often one of the most important—yet often overlooked—sources of support in your quest. In addition to family members and friends, you probably have access to several other individuals who can help you throughout the career decision-making process. These persons might include a career counselor at your college or university, an academic advisor, a favorite teacher, or a recent college graduate.

Each of us will have a different list of individuals who can help us throughout the process of making career decisions. Think about the individuals in your life who can serve as your social support network.

It's also important to consider the many other resources available to you during these latter stages of career decision-making. Exercise 8.3 will help you put together a handy list of all resources, including your social support network, that can aid you during the remaining stages of the career exploration and planning process.

EXERCISE 8.3	*RECOGNIZING RESOURCES*

A. Social Support Network

List below the individuals, including friends, family members, mentors, and anyone else you are aware of (such as a teacher, advisor, career counselor, or religious leader) who you believe will be helpful as you continue the career decision-making process. Below each person's name and telephone number/e-mail address, list the specific ways that person will be able to help you in the process.

NAME:

PHONE NUMBER/E-MAIL:

WAYS THIS PERSON CAN HELP ME:

_____

_____

_____

NAME:

PHONE NUMBER/E-MAIL:

WAYS THIS PERSON CAN HELP ME:

_____

_____

_____

NAME:

PHONE NUMBER/E-MAIL:

WAYS THIS PERSON CAN HELP ME:

_____

_____

_____

NAME:

PHONE NUMBER/E-MAIL:

WAYS THIS PERSON CAN HELP ME:

_____

_____

_____

NAME:

PHONE NUMBER/E-MAIL:

WAYS THIS PERSON CAN HELP ME:

_____

_____

_____

NAME:

PHONE NUMBER/E-MAIL:

WAYS THIS PERSON CAN HELP ME:

_____

_____

_____

NAME:

PHONE NUMBER/E-MAIL:

WAYS THIS PERSON CAN HELP ME:

_____

_____

_____

NAME:

PHONE NUMBER/E-MAIL:

WAYS THIS PERSON CAN HELP ME:

_____

_____

_____

B. Additional Resources

List below all other resources (such as a university career center or public library) that are available as you complete the career decision-making process. Again, list the specific ways that each resource can help.

RESOURCE:

LOCATION:

SPECIFIC WAYS THAT THIS RESOURCE WILL BE HELPFUL:

_____

_____

_____

RESOURCE:

LOCATION:

SPECIFIC WAYS THAT THIS RESOURCE WILL BE HELPFUL:

_____

_____

_____

RESOURCE:

LOCATION:

SPECIFIC WAYS THAT THIS RESOURCE WILL BE HELPFUL:

_____

_____

_____

RESOURCE:

LOCATION:

SPECIFIC WAYS THAT THIS RESOURCE WILL BE HELPFUL:

_____

_____

_____

RESOURCE:

LOCATION:

SPECIFIC WAYS THAT THIS RESOURCE WILL BE HELPFUL:

_____

_____

_____

RESOURCE:

LOCATION:

SPECIFIC WAYS THAT THIS RESOURCE WILL BE HELPFUL:

_____

_____

_____

RESOURCE:

LOCATION:

SPECIFIC WAYS THAT THIS RESOURCE WILL BE HELPFUL:

_____

_____

_____

RESOURCE:

LOCATION:

SPECIFIC WAYS THAT THIS RESOURCE WILL BE HELPFUL:

_____

_____

_____

RESOURCE:

LOCATION:

SPECIFIC WAYS THAT THIS RESOURCE WILL BE HELPFUL:

_____

_____

_____

RESOURCE:

LOCATION:

SPECIFIC WAYS THAT THIS RESOURCE WILL BE HELPFUL:

_____

_____

_____

QUESTIONS FOR CRITICAL THOUGHT

1. Why is it important for you to identify career-related barriers that you may encounter in the future?
2. Why might an individual develop low self-efficacy for overcoming a particular career-related barrier?
3. How can you increase your self-efficacy for overcoming career-related barriers?
4. Why is it important to identify sources of social support during the career decision-making process?

KEY CONCEPTS TO REMEMBER

- Internal barriers come from inside of us, whereas external barriers come from sources outside of us.
- Think about the potential barriers that might develop as you continue the career exploration process.
- Self-efficacy is an individual's confidence in his or her ability to accomplish a specific task.
- If you're confident in your ability to accomplish something, odds are that you will accomplish it.
- Increasing your self-efficacy for overcoming career-related barriers can play an important role in career decision making.
- The social network provided by your friends and family members is one of the most important sources of support in achieving your career goals.

Taking the Leap

MAKING A TENTATIVE CAREER DECISION

Hopefully this book has been useful in helping you narrow down your career choices. If you've completed the activities, done your research, and talked with people in your career fields of choice, you're probably getting excited about one or two specific careers. At the same time, you may be overwhelmed by what making a choice will mean. Some people have difficulty making a decision because they are disappointed that choosing one career will mean dismissing other careers. Other people have difficulty because they cannot picture themselves being successful in a career they still consider fantasy. Here are some important things to remember as you go about making a choice.

- Your decision at this point is still *tentative*. As you progress in your goal setting, you will continually gather new information to incorporate into your career story.

- Jobs are no longer life-long choices. As we've noted throughout this book, the world of work is changing constantly and most people will change jobs and entire careers throughout their lives. Obviously, some careers require a great deal of preparation, which may make it harder to dip in and out of them, but work experience, academic degrees, and on-the-job training are usually marketable in more than one field.

- Most careers rely on a combination of experience, academic training, and skills. While your experience may be weighted in one direction, some new training may help to bridge you into another direction. College majors are a great example of this point. While some majors that are more vocational in nature certainly train you in a particular area, gaining experience in another area will make you marketable in both fields. For example, if you are a computer science major and you have a great deal of retail experience, you could decide to market your degree within the retail industry or you could use your major to be more marketable in the sale of computer equipment. Your major does not lock you into a particular career field.

THE IMPORTANCE OF GOAL SETTING IN CAREER PLANNING

Once you've made a tentative career goal, it is time to start figuring out how you are going to get there. Like the analogy we used in the first chapter, you now have your destination and you have to start mapping your course! If your new career is relatively close to your current career or the job you want is closely related to your major, the map will be fairly short and may include only a couple of turns. If your new career is far away, you will need to plan for some interim goals or stops along the way to ensure good progress. As actor and humorist Will Rogers reminded us, "Even if you're on the right track, you'll get run over if you just sit there."

Using the information about the world of work you are considering and the potential barriers that must be addressed, complete Exercise 9.1 to outline the steps you will need to complete to reach your goal and to be marketable in your new career. If you are still considering more than one career, create a map for each one.

EXERCISE 9.1	*CAREER GOAL MAPPING*

What career field have you tentatively selected? _____

What are the educational/training requirements for this career? _____

_____

Do you currently meet the educational/training requirements for this career? YES NO _____

What are the experience requirements for this career? _____

_____

Do you currently meet the experience requirements for this career? YES NO

_____

What skills will you need to be marketable within this career? _____

_____

Do you currently meet the skills requirements for this career? YES NO

_____

Now we'll need to fill in the gaps by creating a career "to do" list. The following items should be on everyone's career transition list and should always be at the top of your professional development priorities. You will be more successful throughout your professional life if you continually monitor these aspects of your work even if you're in a job you love! If you answered "no" to any of the questions above, add that goal to the bulleted list below.

LONG-TERM CAREER "TO DO" LIST

- Create and expand my network within my career field.

- Create and continually update my resume and cover letter, highlighting the components that make me most marketable within this particular career field.

- Monitor current events in my field so that I can anticipate and prepare for change.

- _____
- _____
- _____
- _____
- _____
- _____

If you are like most people, you'll look at the list you've just created and be slightly overwhelmed. As with any long journey, however, the key is to break down the tasks into smaller, more manageable goals. If you want to get a PhD in molecular biology, you have to start by researching colleges and universities that offer a related major. In other words, think big, but start small! As we've outlined the long-term goals on your list, let's break that down a little bit into manageable steps.

Goals You Hope to Accomplish Within the Next 1–5 years

_____
_____
_____
_____
_____

Goals You Hope to Accomplish Within the Next Year

_____
_____
_____
_____

Goals You Hope to Accomplish Within the Next Six Months

_____
_____
_____
_____

Goals You Hope to Accomplish Within the Next Month

_____

_____

_____

_____

_____

The First Goal I Will Accomplish in Pursuit of This Career

_____

_____

_____

_____

_____

The First Step I Will Take in Accomplishing My First Goal

_____

_____

_____

_____

_____

EDUCATIONAL AND TRAINING OPPORTUNITIES

For some people, career transition will not require any further training or education, but for most people some more school is a necessity. There are many factors to consider when choosing a training program, whether it be vocational/technical training or traditional academic training at a college or university. Refer back to the self-exploration activities you completed in earlier chapters and think about your personal style, interests, values, and life themes as you consider your options. In addition, consider some of the following questions:

Your major does not lock you into a particular career field.

There are many factors to consider when choosing a training program, whether it be vocational/technical training or traditional academic training at a college or university.

■ Mission and Focus: Just as we asked you to think about your life meaning and purpose in Chapter 8, educational institutions have particular goals and missions. Some focus on intellectual knowledge, research, and classic academic pursuits. Others provide specific training programs for working adults designed to prepare you for a particular career. It's important to think about what type of institution will best serve your needs.

■ Academic Training/Focus: Different educational institutions offer different degrees and specializations. Many people believe that most colleges and universities offer similar majors, but there is a great deal of variability. For example, some universities offer agricultural, sports-related, or health-related majors, whereas others do not. If you have a specific degree in mind, make sure that your college of choice offers that degree or a related major.

- Flexibility: If your career choice is still very tentative, be careful not to lock yourself into a particular discipline. For example, if you decide to attend a specific training program for nurses, changing your major may mean transferring schools if you change your mind dramatically. If you're still unsure about your direction, more traditional college campuses may offer the flexibility you need to continue your exploration.

- Resources and Support: Within this exploration stage many people reach out for assistance. Whatever type of training or educational program you decide to enter, ask questions about what type of academic and career support is available.

- Size: While some people thrive on a huge, residential college campus, others prefer a much more intimate setting. Ask yourself what setting you'll need to be in to be successful.

- Location: Are you able to move closer to your program of choice, or do you need to select something within your geographic area?

- Cost: There is a growing crisis in this country related to student debt. Whether this debt is the result of direct costs like tuition and books or indirect needs like housing, students often graduate with huge debts. Be sure to select a training program that is within your budget. Consider meeting with a financial planner to take advantage of as many assistance programs as possible.

- Reputation: While it may sound conceited to say that some degrees or training programs will get you further than others, the fact is that reputation counts. After all, having a degree from Harvard University on the wall of your office instills a certain level of confidence in your customers or clients. In addition to your personal goals and needs, consider who may be the audience for your degree in the future. If you're entering a technical training program to be able to work for a particular company, from what training programs do they recruit? Your research and informational interviewing should help you to answer this question.

- Accessibility: Will you be attending school full-time or do you need a program that will fit around other aspects of your life (e.g., work or family obligations)?

CHOOSING A COLLEGE MAJOR

If you have decided to attend college, or if you are already in college, choosing a major is an important rite of passage. Generally speaking, a college major is a specialization in your academic training designed to complement the more general goals of becoming an educated, thoughtful, problem-solving individual. College majors fall along a continuum from those that are very vocationally oriented (architecture, physical therapy, computer science engineering) to those that are very intellectually and academically oriented (philosophy, religion, psychology). Most majors fall toward the middle of that continuum. Choosing a vocationally oriented major will provide you with more depth of training in that particular career. Choosing an intellectual major provides you with a

A college major is a specialization in your academic training designed to complement the more general goals of becoming an educated, thoughtful, problem-solving individual.

broader education applicable in many career fields. One end of the continuum is no better than the other, simply different.

The process of choosing a major is exactly the same as the process for choosing a career outlined in the first eight chapters of this book—know yourself, know your options, and make a decision. The content is what varies. In addition to the activities in this book, find out more about your academic self by taking introductory courses in diverse fields. Also, talk to academic advisors and career counselors on campus to find out what types of assessments they offer to help you learn more about yourself. When it comes to gathering information about majors, talk to professors and peers majoring in the fields you are considering. Use the "Informational Interviewing Questions" to help you get started. Finally, most college career centers offer information related to what you can do with your major. Visit your career center online or in person to find out what services they have to offer.

TAKING ADVANTAGE OF HAPPENSTANCE . . . A FINAL POINT TO CONSIDER

This book has been focused on purposeful career planning and goal-setting related to careers. The idea is to give you all of the tools that you'll need to be your own best career transition manager. As you will probably have numerous jobs in a number of career fields over your life-span, you should be able to rely on yourself to be your strongest advocate. Developing your career transition skills will help you at every stage, even as you transition into career retirement.

There is one aspect of the career process, however, that we have not yet discussed. Consider some of the people you've interviewed as part of the career decision-making process, or people that you've known over the years. How many of them stumbled upon career opportunities rather than being specifically planful about them? Many people's career stories include some phrase like, "Then, completely by accident I ran into someone who . . ." or "Then I met someone on a plane who told me . . ." or "I happened to read this article and realized . . ." Some people view those occurrences as luck, but as Seneca said in about AD 5, "Luck is what happens when preparation meets opportunity."

Dr. Kathleen Mitchell and Dr. John Krumboltz believe that our culture focuses too much on the idea that career planning should be logical and linear. The idea is that acting on chance occurrences (happenstance) rather than trying to anticipate and micromanage the future leads to greater career satisfaction. With Planned Happenstance, Mitchell advocates a four-step process: explore things you are curious about, remove blocks and obstacles, take advantage of the unexpected, and take action. This is a cyclical process in that continually exploring and removing blocks actually creates opportunities for the unexpected to emerge, leading to new actions. As John Lennon said, "Life is what happens when you're busy making other plans."

CASE STUDIES TO CONSIDER

Diana

Diana was in her last year of her counseling degree and had been planning an internship at an abuse shelter as her last requirement before graduation. Unfortunately, just before she was to begin her internship, the funding was pulled for the program and the shelter was closed. As her graduation depended upon her internship and most positions had already been filled, Diana was desperate to find a position. She was referred to the local career center. When she met with the director to discuss the possibility of an internship, she was quite honest about the fact that she had little interest in career counseling and had not enjoyed her career counseling class very much. She also said, however, that she believed she could learn many skills that would help her in other counseling settings and that she would be dedicated to the internship. The director decided to take a chance on her and allowed her to join the internship program the very next day. Diana soon discovered a passion for working with career clients. She enjoyed the hopeful, positive nature of helping people discover who they are and how they want to impact the world. Putting the counseling theories she had learned in class into practice brought them into a whole new light for her. Midway through her internship, she decided to stay in the field of career counseling and found a position in a career center in the Midwest to pursue after graduation. What began as a desperate compromise turned into a life-changing event for Diana.

Many of the activities advocated in this book, such as informational interviewing and job shadowing, fit into this model well in that they help put you in situations wherein unexpected things can happen. It's up to you to take advantage of them. The Planned Happenstance perspective is actually quite simple: Go out and explore the things you're curious about, and be ready to take advantage of the wonderful things that happen when you put yourself "out there."

> *The Planned Happenstance perspective is actually quite simple: Go out and explore the things you're curious about, and be ready to take advantage of the wonderful things that happen when you put yourself "out there."*

CONCLUSION

Our primary hope in writing this book has been to impart to you the important things to consider when making career decisions and to show you how to engage in the career decision-making process in an effective and satisfying manner. Like any other skills, career management will become easier for you the more you practice.

In particular, we hope you've learned

- That making career decisions requires a comprehensive understanding of who you are—what Super referred to as your self-concept.
- How critical it is that you have a good understanding of your personality, interests, skills, experiences, values, and life themes.
- How to integrate all aspects of your self-concept by articulating your meaning and purpose.
- Using your statement of meaning and purpose when making career decisions, thus maximizing your chances of career satisfaction and success.
- Where to find valuable information when you approach career transitions.
- Valuable ways of thinking about potential barriers to your career choice and methods for overcoming them.
- How understanding these concepts and the career development process will help you take advantage of opportunities, both planned and unplanned, in your career transitions.

Most of all, we hope you've experienced firsthand the fact that investing time and energy in the career decision-making process is well worth the effort.

Throughout this book you have gained tools that will assist you in making career decisions. Use those tools, invest yourself in the process, and you'll surely reap the benefits. Our careers are an integral part of who we are. Make sure that you do all that you can to maximize your chances of career satisfaction and success. If you do, you'll be sure to make career decisions that count!

Appendix A

ENFJ

Communication

- Advertising account executive
- Public relations specialist
- Communication director
- Writer/journalist
- Entertainer/artist
- Fund-raiser
- Recruiter
- Recreational director
- TV producer
- Newscaster
- Politician
- Marketing executive
- Informational-graphics designer
- Editor

Counseling

- Psychologist
- Facilitator
- Career counselor
- Personal counselor
- Clergy/ministry
- Corporate outplacement counselor
- Interpreter/translator
- Alcohol and drug addiction counselor
- Employee assistance counselor

Education/Human Service

- Teacher (health/art/drama/English)
- College professor (humanities)
- Dean of students
- Librarian
- Residential housing director
- Social worker
- Nonprofit organization director
- Special education teacher
- Early education teacher
- Bilingual education teacher
- Child welfare worker
- Social worker (elderly services)

Health Career Services

- Holistic health practitioner (alternative medicine)
- Dietician/nutritionist
- Speech-language pathologist/ audiologist
- Occupational therapist

Business/Consulting

- Human resource development trainer
- Sales trainer
- Recruiter
- Travel agent
- Executive: small business

- Program designer
- Sales manager
- Management consultant: diversity/team building
- Corporate/team trainer
- Outplacement consultant
- Eco-tourism specialist

INFJ

Counseling/Education
- Career counselor
- Psychologist
- Teacher: high school or college English, art, music, social sciences, drama
- Educational consultant
- Librarian
- Special education teacher
- Bilingual education teacher
- Early education teacher
- Employee assistance counselor
- Child welfare counselor
- Alcohol and drug addiction counselor
- Social worker (elderly and child daycare issues)

Religion
- Priest/clergy/monk/nun
- Religious worker
- Director of religious education

Creative
- Artist
- Playwright
- Novelist
- Poet
- Designer
- Informational-graphics designer
- Universal design architect
- Freelance media planner
- Editor/art director
- Genealogist

Health Care/Social Services
- Health care administrator
- Director, social service agency
- Mediator/conflict resolver
- Social scientist
- Social worker
- Mental health counselor
- Dietitian/nutritionist
- Speech-language pathologist/audiologist
- Holistic health practitioner (alternative medicine)
- Massage therapist
- Occupational therapist

Business
- Human resources manager
- Marketer (of ideas and/or services)
- Organizational development consultant
- Employee assistance program coordinator/counselor
- Job analyst
- Diversity manager-human resources
- Corporate/team trainer
- Preferred customer sales representative
- Merchandise planner
- Environmental lawyer
- Interpreter/translator

ENFP

Creative
- Journalist
- Screenwriter/playwright
- Columnist
- Character actor
- Musician/composer
- Newscaster
- Interior decorator
- Cartoonist
- Artist
- Reporter/editor
- Informational-graphics designer

Marketing/Planning
- Public relations specialist
- Marketing consultant
- Advertising account executive

- Copy writer/publicity writer
- Advertising creative director
- Strategic planner
- Publicist
- Research assistant
- Editor/art director

Education/Counseling

- Special education teacher
- Bilingual education teacher
- Early childhood education teacher
- Teacher: art/drama/music/English
- Child welfare counselor
- Alcohol/drug addiction counselor
- Social worker (elderly and child care issues)
- Development director
- Career counselor
- Residential housing director
- Ombudsperson
- Pastoral counselor
- Rehabilitation worker
- Social scientist
- Psychologist

Health Care/Social Service

- Dietician/nutritionist
- Speech-language pathologist/audiologist
- Holistic health practitioner (alternative medicine)

- Massage therapist
- Employee assistance program counselor
- Physical therapist
- Legal mediator

Entrepreneurial/Business

- Consultant
- Inventor
- Sales: intangibles/ideas
- Human resources manager
- Human resources development trainer
- Conference planner
- Employment development specialist
- Restaurateur
- Management consultant: change management/team building/diversity
- Merchandise planner
- Diversity manager—human resources
- Corporate/team trainer
- Advertising account manager or account executive
- Public relations specialist
- Marketing executive: radio/TV/cable broadcast industry
- Outplacement consultant
- Environmental attorney

INFP

Creative/Arts

- Artist
- Writer: poet/novelist
- Journalist
- Entertainer
- Architect
- Actor
- Editor
- Musician
- Informational-graphics designer
- Editor/art director

Education/Counseling

- College professor: humanities/arts
- Researcher
- Psychologist
- Counselor

- Social worker
- Librarian
- Educational consultant
- Special education teacher
- Bilingual education teacher
- Early childhood education teacher
- Employee assistance counselor
- Child welfare counselor
- Alcohol and drug addiction counselor
- Social worker (elderly and child care issues)
- Translator/interpreter
- Legal mediator

Religion

- Minister/priest
- Religious educator

- Missionary
- Church worker

Health Care
- Dietician/nutritionist
- Physical therapist
- Home health social worker
- Occupational therapist
- Speech-language pathologist/ audiologist
- Massage therapist

- Holistic health practitioner (alternative medicine)

Organizational Development
- Employee development specialist
- Human resources development specialist
- Social scientist
- Diversity manager
- Consultant: team building/conflict resolution

ENTJ

Business
- Executive
- Senior manager
- Office manager
- Administrator
- Personnel manager
- Sales manager
- Marketing manager
- Network integration specialist (telecommunications)
- Technical trainer
- Information services: new business developer
- Logistics consultant (manufacturing)
- Management consultant: computer/ information services, marketing, reorganization
- Advertising account manager
- Marketing executive: radio/TV/cable broadcast industry
- Media planner/buyer
- International sales and marketing
- Franchise owner
- Sales manager: pharmaceuticals
- Administrator: health services

Finance
- Personal financial planner
- Economic analyst
- Mortgage broker

- Credit investigator
- Stockbroker
- Investment banker
- Corporate finance attorney
- International banker
- Economist

Consulting/Training
- Business consultant
- Management consultant
- Educational consultant
- Program designer
- Management trainer
- Employment development specialist
- Labor relations
- Telecommunications security consultant
- Corporate team trainer

Professional
- Attorney
- Judge
- Psychologist
- Science/social science teacher
- Chemical engineer
- Intellectual property attorney
- Biomedical engineer
- Psychiatrist
- Environmental engineer

INTJ

Business/Finance
- Telecommunications security
- Management consultant: computer information services, marketing, reorganization

- Economist
- International banker
- Pharmaceutical researcher (R&D)
- Financial planner
- Investment banker

Technical
- Scientist/scientific researcher
- Computer systems analyst
- Technician: electrical/electronic
- Design engineer
- Astronomer
- Computer programmer
- Environmental planner
- Biomedical researcher/engineer
- Computer systems analyst
- Information services developer
- Software and systems researcher and developer
- Information services: new business developer
- Network integration specialist (telecommunications)

Education
- Teacher: university
- Academic curriculum designer
- Administrator
- Mathematician

Health Care/Medicine
- Psychiatrist
- Psychologist
- Neurologist
- Biomedical engineer

- Cardiologist
- Pharmacologist
- Pharmaceutical researcher
- Biomedical researcher

Professional
- Attorney: administrative/litigator
- Management consultation
- Strategic planner
- Investment/business analyst
- Manager
- Judge
- News analyst/writer
- Engineer
- Metallurgical engineer
- Intellectual properties attorney
- Civil engineer

Creative
- Writer/editorial writer
- Artist
- Inventor
- Designer
- Architect
- Universal design architect
- Informational-graphics designer
- Freelance media planner
- Editor/art director

ENTP

Politics
- Politician
- Political manager
- Political analyst
- Social scientist

Planning and Development
- Strategic planner
- Personnel systems developer
- Real estate agent/developer
- Special projects developer
- Investment broker
- Computer analyst
- Industrial design manager
- Logistics consultant (manufacturing)
- Network integration specialist (telecommunications)
- Financial planner
- Investment banker

Marketing/Creative
- Advertising creative director
- Public relations specialist
- Marketing researcher/planner
- Sports marketing
- Radio/TV talk show host
- Producer
- Art director
- International marketing
- Informational-graphics designer
- New business development: information services

Entrepreneurship/Business
- Entrepreneur
- Inventor
- Management consultant
- Venture capitalist
- Literary agent

- Photographer
- Journalist
- Owner: restaurant/bar
- Actor
- Outplacement consultant

- Technical trainer
- Diversity manager/trainer
- Management consultant: marketing/reorganization/compensation

INTP

Planning and Development
- Software designer
- Computer programmer
- Research and development specialist
- Systems analyst/database manager
- Strategic planner
- New market or product conceptualizer
- Information services developer: computer programming
- Information services: new business developer
- Network integration specialist (telecommunications)
- Change management consultant
- Financial planner
- Investment banker
- Management consultant: computer/information services, marketing, re-organization

Health Care/Technical
- Neurologist
- Physicist
- Plastic surgeon
- Pharmacist
- Scientist: chemistry/biology
- Pharmaceutical researcher
- Biomedical engineer/researcher
- Veterinarian

Professional
- Lawyer
- Economist

- Psychologist/psychoanalyst
- Financial analyst
- Architect
- Investigator
- Intellectual property attorney
- Legal mediator
- Corporate financial attorney
- Psychiatrist

Academic
- Mathematician
- Archaeologist
- Historian
- Philosopher
- College teacher of advanced students
- Researcher
- Logician
- College faculty administrator
- Economist
- Interpreter/translator

Creative
- Photographer
- Creative writer
- Artist
- Entertainer/dancer
- Musician
- Agent
- Inventor
- Informational-graphics designer

ESTJ

Sales/Service
- Insurance agent
- Sales (tangibles): computers, real estate
- Funeral director
- Cook

- Military officer
- Teacher: trade, industrial, technical
- Government employee
- Security guard
- Sports merchandise/equipment sales
- Pharmaceutical sales

- Telecommunications security
- Police/probation/corrections officer

Technical/Physical
- Engineer: mechanical/applied fields
- Computer analyst
- Auditor
- General contractor
- Farmer
- Construction worker
- Pharmacist
- Clinical technician
- Accounting internal auditor
- Technical trainer
- EEG technologist/technician
- Paralegal

Managerial
- Bank officer/loan officer
- Project manager
- Office manager
- Administrator
- Factory supervisor
- Database manager
- Purchasing agent
- Credit analyst

- Regulatory compliance officer
- Budget analyst
- Administrator: health services
- Chief information officer
- Management consultant: business operations
- Logistics and supply manager
- Bank manager/loan officer
- Credit analyst/counselor

Professional
- Dentist
- Physician: general medicine
- Stockbroker
- Judge
- Executive
- Teacher: technical trades
- Civil/mechanical/metallurgical engineer
- Corporate finance lawyer
- Electrical engineer
- Primary care physician
- Industrial engineer
- Paralegal
- Pharmacist

ISTJ

Business
- Auditor
- Office manager
- Accountant
- Manager/supervisor
- Word processing specialist
- Efficiency expert/analyst
- Insurance underwriter
- Logistics and supply manager
- Regulatory compliance officer
- Chief information officer
- Accountant/actuary

Sales/Service
- Police officer/detective
- IRS agent
- Government employee
- Military officer
- Corrections sergeant
- Real estate agent

- Sports equipment/merchandise sales
- Corrections officer

Finance
- Bank examiner
- Investment securities officer
- Tax examiner
- Stockbroker
- Estate planner
- Credit analyst
- Budget analyst

Education
- School principal
- Teacher: technical/industrial/math/ physical education
- Librarian
- Administrator

Legal/Technical
- Law researcher
- Legal secretary
- Electrician

- Engineer
- Mechanic
- Computer programmer
- Technical writer
- Legal secretary/paralegal
- Pharmaceutical sales/researcher
- EEG technologist/technician
- Geologist
- Meteorologist
- Airline mechanic
- Mechanical/industrial/electrical engineer
- Agricultural scientist

Health Care
- Veterinarian
- General surgeon
- Dentist
- Nursing administrator
- Health care administrator
- Pharmacist
- Lab technologist
- Medical researcher
- Primary care physician
- Biomedical technologist
- Exercise physiologist
- Pharmacist/pharmacy technician

ESFJ

Health Career Services
- Medical/dental assistant
- Speech pathologist
- Exercise physiologist
- Family physician
- Nurse
- Dentist
- Medical secretary
- Optometrist
- Dietician/nutritionist
- Massage therapist
- Optometrist/optician
- Pharmacist/pharmacy technician
- Respiratory therapist
- Veterinarian
- Licensed practical nurse (LPN)
- Home health aid
- Primary care physician
- Physical therapist
- Home health social worker

Education
- Elementary school teacher
- Special education teacher
- Child care provider
- Home economics teacher
- Athletic coach
- Bilingual education teacher

Social Service/Counseling
- Social worker
- Community welfare worker
- Professional volunteer
- Religious educator

- Counselor
- Minister/priest/rabbi
- Employee assistance counselor
- Child welfare counselor
- Alcohol and drug addiction counselor
- Social worker (elderly and child care issues)
- Paralegal

Business
- Public relations account executive
- Personal banker
- Sales representative (tangibles)
- Telemarketer
- Office manager
- Retail owner/operator
- Receptionist
- Management consultant: human resources/training
- Insurance agent (families)
- Credit counselor
- Merchandise planner

Sales/Services
- Flight attendant
- Customer services representative
- Funeral home director
- Hairdresser/cosmetologist
- Host/hostess
- Caterer
- Fundraiser
- Travel sales
- Ecotourism specialist
- Real estate agent/broker

- Marketing executive: radio/TV/cable/ broadcast industry
- Translator/interpreter
- Genealogist
- Home health care sales
- Sports equipment/merchandise sales

Clerical
- Secretary
- Receptionist
- Office machine operator
- Bookkeeper
- Typist

ISFJ

Health Care
- Dental hygienist
- Family physician
- Nurse
- Medical technologist
- Physical therapist
- Medical equipment sales
- Health care administrator
- Dietician/nutritionist
- Optician
- Medical records administrator
- Pharmacist/pharmacy technician
- Radiological technician
- Respiratory therapist
- Veterinarian
- Licensed practical nurse (LPN)
- Primary care physician
- Home health aid
- Medical/dental assistant

Social Service/Education
- Preschool/elementary teacher
- Librarian/archivist
- Curator
- Educational administrator
- Social worker
- Guidance counselor
- Personal counselor
- Religious educator
- Speech pathologist
- Probation officer
- Home health social worker
- Child welfare counselor
- Alcohol and drug addiction counselor

- Social worker (elderly and child care issues)
- Elementary school teacher
- Special education teacher
- Librarian/archivist
- Genealogist
- Curator
- Educational administrator
- Guidance counselor
- Religious educator
- Social worker (elderly services)

Business
- Secretary
- Clerical supervisor
- Customer service representative
- Personnel administrator
- Computer operator
- Bookkeeper
- Credit counselor
- Paralegal
- Home health care sales

Creative/Technical
- Interior decorator
- Electrician
- Retail owner
- Innkeeper
- Artist
- Musician
- Preferred customer sales representative
- Merchandise planner
- Real estate agent/broker

ESTP

Sales/Service/"Action"
- Police officer
- Firefighter

- Paramedic
- Detective
- Pilot

- Investigator
- Corrections officer
- Real estate agent
- Emergency medical technician
- Exercise physiologist/sports medicine
- Respiratory therapist
- Flight attendant
- Sports merchandise sales
- Insurance fraud investigator
- Private investigator/detective

Finance
- Personal financial planner
- Auditor
- Stockbroker
- Banker
- Investor
- Insurance sales
- Budget analyst
- Insurance agent/broker (sales)

Entertainment/Sports
- Sportscaster
- News reporter
- Promoter
- Tour agent
- Dancer
- Bartender
- Auctioneer
- Professional athlete/coach
- Fitness instructor/trainer

Technical/Trade
- Carpenter
- Craftsperson/artisan
- Farmer
- General contractor
- Construction worker
- Chef/cook
- Electrical engineer
- Electronics specialist
- Technical trainer: classroom setting
- Logistics and supply manager: manufacturing
- Network integration specialist (telecommunications)
- Civil engineer (repairs of transportation infrastructure)
- Industrial/mechanical engineer
- Surveyor
- EEG technologist/technician
- Radiological technician
- Aircraft mechanic
- Marine biologist

Business
- Real estate broker/agent
- Entrepreneur
- Land developer
- Wholesaler
- Retail sales
- Car sales
- Management consultant (business operations)
- Franchise owner

ISTP

Sales/Service/Corrections
- Police/corrections officer
- Race car driver
- Pilot
- Weapons operator
- Hunter
- Intelligence agent
- Marshal
- Firefighter
- Surveyor
- Sports equipment/merchandise sales
- Pharmaceutical sales
- Private investigator/detective

Technical
- Electrical/mechanical/civil engineer
- Electronics specialist
- Technical trainer: one-to-one setting
- Information services developer
- Software developer
- Logistics and supply manager: manufacturer
- Network integration specialist (telecommunications)
- Computer programmer
- Marine biologist

Health Career Services
- EEG technologist/technician
- Radiological technician
- Emergency medical technician
- Exercise physiologist
- Dental assistant/hygienist

Business/Finance
- Securities analyst
- Purchasing agent
- Office manager
- Banker
- Economist

- Legal secretary
- Management consultant (business operations)
- Paralegal

Trades
- Computer repair person
- Airline mechanic
- Farmer
- Coach/trainer
- Carpenter
- Automotive products retailer
- Commercial artist

ESFP

Education/Social Service
- Teacher: early childhood and elementary
- Child care provider
- Athletic coach
- Home health social worker
- Special education teacher
- Alcohol and drug addiction counselor
- Child welfare counselor
- Marine biologist

Health Care
- Emergency room nurse
- Social worker
- Dog obedience trainer
- Medical assistant
- Dental assistant and hygienist
- Licensed practical nurse
- Physical therapist
- Primary care physician
- Home health aid
- Massage therapist
- Dietitian/nutritionist
- Optician/optometrist
- Emergency medical technician
- Exercise physiologist
- Pharmacy technician
- Radiological technician
- Respiratory therapist
- Veterinarian/veterinary technician
- Occupational therapist

Entertainment
- Travel agent/tour operator
- Photographer
- Film producer
- Musician
- Performer: dancer, comedian
- Promoter
- Special events coordinator

Business/Sales
- Retail merchandiser/planner
- Public relations specialist
- Fundraiser
- Labor relations mediator
- Receptionist
- Merchandise planner
- Diversity manager: human resources
- Team trainer
- Travel sales
- Insurance agent/broker (health or life)
- Real estate agent
- Sports equipment sales/marketing
- Retail sales/management
- Home health care sales

Service
- Flight attendant
- Secretary/receptionist
- Waiter/waitress
- Host/hostess
- Floral designer
- Police/corrections officer (specialty in remedial training, rehabilitation, counseling)

ISFP

Crafts/Artisan

- Fashion designer
- Carpenter
- Jeweler
- Gardener
- Tapestry worker
- Potter
- Painter
- Dancer
- Designer: interior/landscape
- Chef

Health Care

- Visiting nurse
- Physical therapist
- Massage therapist
- Radiology technologist
- Medical assistant
- Dental assistant/hygienist
- Veterinary assistant
- Animal groomer/trainer
- Home health aid
- Primary care physician
- Dietitian/nutritionist
- Optician/optometrist
- Exercise physiologist
- Occupational therapist
- Art therapist
- Pharmacy technician
- Respiratory therapist
- Licensed practical nurse

Technical

- Surveyor
- Computer operator

- Forester
- Botanist
- Geologist
- Mechanic
- Marine biologist

Sales/Service

- Teacher: elementary (science/art)
- Police/corrections officer
- Crisis hotline operator
- Storekeeper
- Waiter/waitress
- Beautician
- Travel sales
- Preferred customer sales representative
- Merchandise planner
- Sports equipment sales
- Home health care sales
- Home health social worker
- Child welfare counselor
- Alcohol and drug addiction counselor
- Social worker (elderly and child care issues)

Business

- Bookkeeper
- Legal secretary
- Typist
- Clerical supervisor
- Administrator
- Paralegal

Appendix B

EXERCISE 2.1: What's My Type? and

EXERCISE 3.2: Career Dreaming

To score Exercises 2.1 and 3.2, you'll need to determine which "work environment" best describes each of the careers included on your list. "Work environment" refers to Dr. Roe's categories for describing career types: Service, Business Contact, Organization, Technology, Outdoors, Science, General Culture, and Arts and Entertainment. Refer to Chapter 6 for Dr. Roe's classification system.

Next to each of the careers included in your lists in Exercises 2.1 and 3.2, write the work environment type that *best* describes that particular career. If you're unable to determine which work environment is most appropriate for a particular career, you might ask a career counselor or teacher for some advice or consult Appendix C for a list of careers arranged by occupational type.

An example might help to clarify this scoring procedure. Suppose one of the careers you might include on your Dream List would be "actor." Because being an actor involves artistic talent and creativity, and because the description of the Arts and Entertainment work environment is the best description of the types of things an actor is involved in, you would write ARTS AND ENTERTAINMENT next to "actor" on your Dream List. Another career you might include on your Dream List might be pediatrician. If you weren't sure which work environment is associated with being a pediatrician, you could turn to Appendix C. Referring to Appendix C, you'd discover that the appropriate occupational type for pediatrician is Science. If you're unable to figure out the appropriate career type for a particular career you're considering, ask an instructor, career counselor, or adviser for some guidance.

Go ahead now and write the primary occupational type (Service, Business Contact, Organization, Technology, Outdoors, Science, General Culture, or Arts and Entertainment) next to each of the careers in your lists from Exercises 2.1 and 3.2.

Next, fill in the "scores" for each work environment category by awarding 5 points for each occurrence of the occupational types included in your lists. For example, if your list of careers generated from Exercise 2.1 included one Arts and Entertainment career, four Service careers, and three Science careers, you'd award 5 points to Arts and Entertainment (because your list included one Arts and Entertainment career), 20 points to Service, and 15 points to Science. Your scores for this exercise would look like this:

SCORES FROM EXERCISE 2.1

Service	Business Contact	Organization	Technology	Outdoors	Science	General Culture	Arts & Entertainment
20	0	0	0	0	15	0	5

Repeat this process for assigning scores to each of the career types for Exercise 3.2.

EXERCISE 3.3: Activities Ratings

This exercise also results in a score for each of the work environments. The total score for each type is determined by adding together the ratings you assigned to each of the activities representing a particular occupational type. Your Service score, for example, is the sum of your ratings for the five Service types of activities included in Exercise 3.3.

The guide shown below indicates which items in Exercise 3.3 represent each work environment. For example, item numbers 5, 8, 26, 32, and 39 represent service careers. Above each item number, fill in the ratings you gave the item in Exercise 3.3. Then simply add up your scores in each occupational category to determine your total scores. Each total score should be somewhere between 5 and 25 points. Place the score for each career type in the appropriate spaces in Exercise 6.2.

SERVICE:

_____ + _____ + _____ + _____ + _____ = _____
  5   8   26   32   39

BUSINESS CONTACT:

_____ + _____ + _____ + _____ + _____ = _____
  2   12   24   33   36

ORGANIZATION:

_____ + _____ + _____ + _____ + _____ = _____
  3   11   14   18   22

TECHNOLOGY:

_____ + _____ + _____ + _____ + _____ = _____
  15   21   27   35   40

OUTDOORS:

_____ + _____ + _____ + _____ + _____ = _____
  6   10   16   30   38

SCIENCE:

_____ + _____ + _____ + _____ + _____ = _____
  1   7   17   20   25

GENERAL CULTURE:

_____ + _____ + _____ + _____ + _____ = _____
  4   13   19   29   37

ARTS AND ENTERTAINMENT:

_____ + _____ + _____ + _____ + _____ = _____
  9   23   28   31   34

EXERCISE 3.4: Linking the Past to the Present

To score this exercise, follow the same procedure as for scoring Exercise 3.3. The guide shown below indicates which items in Exercise 3.4 represent each career type. As you did for Exercise 3.3, add up the ratings for each type and record them in the appropriate spaces in Exercise 6.2.

SERVICE:

_____ + _____ + _____ + _____ + _____ = _____
  2   10   17   25   36

BUSINESS CONTACT:

_____ + _____ + _____ + _____ + _____ = _____
  3   13   23   28   37

ORGANIZATION:

_____ + _____ + _____ + _____ + _____ = _____
  7   20   24   29   35

TECHNOLOGY:

_____ + _____ + _____ + _____ + _____ = _____
  6   21   26   34   38

OUTDOORS:

_____ + _____ + _____ + _____ + _____ = _____
  4   12   15   30   39

SCIENCE:

_____ + _____ + _____ + _____ + _____ = _____
  5   11   18   22   32

GENERAL CULTURE:

_____ + _____ + _____ + _____ + _____ = _____
  8   16   27   31   40

ARTS AND ENTERTAINMENT:

_____ + _____ + _____ + _____ + _____ = _____
  1   9   14   19   33

EXERCISE 3.5: How Well Do You Do What You Do?

As you did for Exercises 3.3 and 3.4, you simply need to determine the total rating points for the skills representing each career type. The guide shown below indicates which skill items in Exercise 3.5 represent each career type. Record the total scores for each type in the appropriate spaces in Exercise 6.2.

SERVICE:

_____ + _____ + _____ + _____ + _____ = _____
1   13   17   23   30

BUSINESS CONTACT:

_____ + _____ + _____ + _____ + _____ = _____
5   15   25   35   39

ORGANIZATION:

_____ + _____ + _____ + _____ + _____ = _____
4   9   16   20   29

TECHNOLOGY:

_____ + _____ + _____ + _____ + _____ = _____
10   18   26   33   37

OUTDOORS:

_____ + _____ + _____ + _____ + _____ = _____
2   8   24   31   38

SCIENCE:

_____ + _____ + _____ + _____ + _____ = _____
12   21   27   32   36

GENERAL CULTURE:

_____ + _____ + _____ + _____ + _____ = _____
3   7   19   22   28

ARTS AND ENTERTAINMENT:

_____ + _____ + _____ + _____ + _____ = _____
6   11   14   34   40

Appendix C

OCCUPATIONS ARRANGED BY WORK ENVIRONMENT

Service

Barber
Bartender
Career counselor
Chef
Child care worker
Clinical psychologist
Correctional officer
Counseling psychologist
Counselor (general)
Day care worker
Dental assistant
Detective
Dietician/nutritionist
Emergency medical technician
FBI agent
Firefighter
Flight attendant
Food service worker
Hairdresser

Highway patrol officer
Homemaker
Hospital attendant
Lifeguard
Occupational therapist
Physical therapist
Police officer
Police sergeant
Practical nurse
Prison guard
Probation officer
Psychotherapist
Religious worker
Server (restaurant)
Sheriff
Social worker
Taxi driver
Teacher's aide
YMCA/YWCA director

Business Contact

Advertising executive
Auctioneer
Automobile salesperson

Insurance salesperson
Insurance agent/broker
Marketing professional

Mortgage broker
Promoter
Public relations specialist
Real estate agent

Retail/wholesale dealer
Sales representative
Traveling salesperson

Organization

Accountant
Actuary
Administrative assistant
Armed services officer
Auditor
Banker
Bank teller
Bookkeeper
Business executive
Business manager
Buyer
Cashier
Certified public accountant
Chief executive officer
Clerical supervisor
Court reporter
Department store clerk
Employment manager
Financial manager
Financial planner
General office clerk
Government executive
Health administrator
Hotel clerk
Hotel manager

Human resources director
Management consultant
Medical records technician
Office clerk
Office manager
Payroll clerk
Personnel manager
Politician
Postal worker
Public official
Purchasing agent
Receptionist
Restaurant manager
Retail sales manager
Sales clerk
Sales manager
Secretary
Shipping and receiving clerk
Small business owner
Statistician
Stenographer
Stockbroker
Typist
Warehouse supervisor
Word processing specialist

Technology

Aerospace engineer
Aircraft mechanic
Applied scientist
Auto body repairer
Automobile mechanic
Aviator/pilot
Bricklayer
Building contractor
Bus driver

Butcher
Carpenter
Chemical engineer
Civil engineer
Computer repairer
Construction worker
Draftsperson
Electrician
Electronics equipment repairer

Engineer (general)
Engineering technician
Engine mechanic
Factory worker
Farm equipment mechanic
General repairperson
Heating, air conditioning, and
    refrigeration technician
Heavy equipment specialist
Jeweler
Machinist
Mechanic

Mechanical engineer
Painter
Pipefitter
Plumber
Printer
Printing press operator
Sheet metal worker
Steel worker
Tailor
Truck driver
Welder

Outdoors

Agricultural specialist
Agronomist
Botanist
Dairy hand
Farmer
Floriculturalist
Forest ranger
Game warden

Gardener
Horticulturalist
Landscape architect
Land surveyor
Rancher
Tractor driver
Tree surgeon
Wildlife specialist

Science

Anthropologist
Archaeologist
Astronomer
Audiologist
Biochemist
Biologist
Cardiologist
Chemist
Chiropractor
Dentist
Experimental psychologist
Laboratory technician
Life scientist
Mathematician
Medical specialist
Medical technician
Meteorologist
Neurologist

Nurse
Obstetrician
Oceanographer
Ophthalmologist
Optometrist
Paleontologist
Pathologist
Pediatrician
Pharmacist
Physician
Physicist
Podiatrist
Psychiatrist
Psychologist
Radiologist
Research scientist
Science teacher
Sociologist

Speech pathologist

Surgeon

University/college professor
(science field)

Veterinarian

X-ray technician

General Culture

Broadcaster

Clergy (minister, rabbi, priest)

Editor

Educational administrator

Elementary school teacher

High school teacher

Historian

Interpreter

Journalist

Judge

Law clerk

Lawyer

Librarian

Newscaster

News commentator

Paralegal assistant

Philosopher

Preschool teacher

Radio announcer

Reporter

School principal

School superintendent

Social scientist

Teacher

University/college professor

Urban planner

Arts and Entertainment

Actor

Advertising artist

Advertising writer

Architect

Art teacher

Art critic

Artist

Athletic coach

Author/writer

Choreographer

Cinematographer

Commercial artist

Composer

Cosmetologist

Dance instructor

Dancer

Designer

Drama teacher

Entertainer

Fine artist

Graphic designer

Interior decorator

Music arranger

Musician

Performing artist

Photographer

Professional athlete

Race car driver

Screenwriter

Sculptor

Singer

Stage design

Appendix D

Probably the most important thing to remember about job search strategies is that the more strategies you're willing to use, the better your chances are for locating the type of job you really want. By expanding your job search strategies to include multiple sources, you increase your chances of finding out about a significantly greater number of jobs. The following list provides you with information about several resources available to help you when seeking part-time, volunteer, or full-time employment.

CLASSIFIED ADVERTISEMENTS

Many people find out about job openings by reading the classified ads in their newspapers. In large towns, hundreds and sometimes thousands of jobs in a variety of fields are listed in each week's Sunday paper. These job opportunities are arranged alphabetically by job type and can provide you with a quick reference to job openings. Even in smaller towns, many openings are listed in the classified ads. If you're hoping to work somewhere other than where you're currently living, you should check the classified ads of the newspaper published in that particular city.

With the advent of the Internet, many newspapers provide online access to the classified ads section. If you're not sure whether your city's newspaper is accessible online, try calling the newspaper's editorial offices or using a search engine to search for it. Remember that classified job listings represent only a very small percentage of existing job openings. That's why you'll want to use a variety of other resources when searching for a job.

YOUR NETWORK OF CONNECTIONS

These days, with increased competition for jobs, many people realize that their personal and professional connections often play an important role in securing a job. The more people you know who are willing to help you locate the type of job you're seeking, the better off you'll be. The time to begin making these connections is now—well before you're ready to begin working full-time in your career field. Your network of connections can include friends, family members, community and religious leaders, and other persons who can help you locate openings.

TEACHERS AND COUNSELORS

High school teachers and college professors who are active in their communities are often valuable sources for identifying employment opportunities related to your career. You might try asking some of your teachers for information. At the very least, they may be able to point you in certain directions that will increase your chances of finding a good job. Career counselors can also be a source of information about employment opportunities. In addition to offering the same type of help teachers and professors can provide, career counselors—especially those who work at college and university career centers—often receive job announcements. Check with your career center to find out whether such announcements are available and whether they're accessible online.

JOB POSTINGS

Many jobs that are available in a community are included in job postings, lists of openings (often in both hard copy and via the Internet) within a company or an organization. Most college and university career planning and placement centers post jobs online. Most large companies have a link to openings on their company home pages.

CAREER FAIRS

Career fairs are large organized gatherings of several employers who are looking for new employees to join their companies. These fairs are usually organized by high schools, colleges, and universities or by large civic and community groups. In large cities, newspapers often sponsor career fairs as well. Career fairs are a good way to find out which companies are hiring in your area and what opportunities exist in other regions of the country. If you attend a career fair, dress appropriately and take copies of your resume.

ONLINE JOB LISTINGS

Finding large numbers of job postings online isn't difficult. Sites such as www.monster.com, www.hotjobs.com, and www.careerbuilder.com are easily searchable and can provide you with many listings to wade through. Some people are overwhelmed by the volume of postings on these sites. Sometimes it helps to use the large search engines to figure out who is hiring in your area and then go directly to that company's Web site to apply.

ONE-STOP CAREER CENTERS

Because of the focus on school-to-work transitions in recent years, many county and state government agencies have established "one-stop career centers." One-stop career centers help members of the community with all stages of the career decision-making process. The focus of such centers, however, is usually to assist individuals who are looking for jobs in the area. See whether there is a one-stop career center in your community. Just about any college or university career center should be able to tell you whether one is available.

EMPLOYMENT AGENCIES

Although at one time employment agencies and "headhunters" were commonly used in finding a job, these organizations are used much less now. Nevertheless, you might want to find out if an employment agency can help you locate job openings related to your career choice. Keep in mind, however, that some employment agencies charge a fee for their services, whereas most of the other sources listed in this chapter are free. Employment agencies are almost always listed in the phone book under "Employment." You might also want to consider talking with a temporary employment agency. What many people don't realize is that temporary agencies often help people find long-term, full-time employment. Furthermore, temporary situations often turn into permanent ones.

JOB APPLICATION PROCEDURES

Different jobs require different application procedures. Be sure to follow all application guidelines *strictly*. If an employer states in an advertisement that resumes should be sent and that no phone calls will be accepted, you should send your resume (along with a cover letter, of course) and *not* call the company. Although following directions may seem like common sense, we've had many clients over the years tell us that they always thought it would be a good idea to call the company anyway—even though the advertisement for the position said only to send a resume. Think about it for a moment: If you were an employer, would you want to hire someone who followed directions, or someone who decided to do it some other way instead?

Most jobs require prospective employees to complete an application form. If you can complete the application at home, by all means do so. If you have access to a typewriter, the application should definitely be typed. If a typewriter isn't available, *very neatly* print all of your information. If you must complete the application on site, use a ballpoint pen (blue or black ink) unless otherwise directed. Take your time to complete the form neatly and accurately. It's also a good idea to dress appropriately when completing an application on site, even if a job interview won't be conducted at that time. The first impression you make is often a lasting one.

Be sure you have all of the necessary information with you in case you have to complete applications there. Take a copy of your resume with you. Information that is routinely requested on job applications is listed below.

Job Application Information

YOUR NAME, MAILING ADDRESS, TELEPHONE NUMBER, AND E-MAIL ADDRESS

In addition to providing your current contact information, you might also be asked to list your previous home address and phone number—especially if you've been living at your current residence for less than two years.

EDUCATIONAL BACKGROUND

Most applications require you to list high school and college information, including names, addresses, and telephone numbers of the institutions you attended. You also may be asked to indicate how many hours of course work you've completed at each educational level and what type of diploma, degree, or certificate was awarded to you. Dates of graduation and/or certification will be requested on most applications.

PREVIOUS WORK EXPERIENCES

Even if you have a resume available, many employers will still want you to list your previous work experiences on the official application. You'll need to have the starting and ending dates of your previous employment, the names and addresses of the companies or organizations you worked for, the names and phone numbers of your immediate supervisors, and a brief description of the work-related responsibilities associated with each job. You may also be asked to provide your salary history. Applications often require you to list both your starting and ending salary for each of your previous jobs.

PERSONAL AND PROFESSIONAL REFERENCES

Most applications request contact information (names, addresses, phone numbers and e-mail addresses) for both personal and professional references. Personal references are those people you would consider friends. The personal references you list on a job application should be people who know you quite well on an interpersonal level. Professional references can include former supervisors, teachers, or even coworkers who can attest to the quality of your work. Make sure you have handy all of the contact information for at least four or five personal and four or five professional references so that you can fully complete an application. Be sure to request permission to use personal and professional contacts as references.

MISCELLANEOUS INFORMATION

Depending on the application, you might be asked to provide a variety of additional information, ranging from a list of your hobbies and interests to previous awards you've received and special talents and skills you possess.

YOUR ONLINE PROFILE

Before you begin your job search, review your online profile. Employers use the Internet to learn more about their candidates, and you want to be sure that there is nothing online that will at a minimum embarrass you and at a maximum keep you from getting a job or internship. If you have your own Web site, are often included on friends' Web sites, or use social networking sites like MySpace or FaceBook, you probably have a great deal of information online. Go to a regular search engine such as Google or Yahoo! and do a search on your name. If you wouldn't want an employer to see what you find, try to get it cleaned up as soon as possible. If you don't own the Web site, it may not be easy to do, so start early.

THE EMPLOYMENT INTERVIEW

Probably the best job interview strategy that anyone could suggest is for you to attend a workshop on job-interviewing skills. Most college and university career centers offer interviewing skills workshops that can be especially effective for persons who lack interviewing experience. Some of these workshops even provide a videotaping service, in which a mock interview is taped so that you can see how you interact with someone during an interview situation. If you're unable to attend a workshop, at the very least you should practice with a friend or family member. After running through a few "trials," you'll be much more prepared for an actual interview.

Another important point to consider is *always* to dress as professionally as possible when interviewing for a job—even for jobs that don't have strict dress codes. As mentioned before, the first impression you'll make with a prospective employer is going to last a long time. When hundreds of people are applying for a limited number of jobs, *everything* that you say and do plays an important role in whether you are offered the job.

It's also a good idea to go to an interview well prepared. Researching the company, for example, can give you a sense of what direction the company is moving in. This might help you anticipate the kinds of questions that you'll be asked during the interview. It also helps you come up with something interesting and meaningful to say when the interviewer asks you whether *you* have any questions about the company or the position.

Make sure you'll be able to find the location of the interview before the day of your appointment. The last thing you want to do on your way to an interview is get lost. By finding out well in advance precisely where your interview is going to be held, you'll decrease some of the anxiety that's a natural part of interviewing.

Preparation is the key to successful job search strategies and application procedures. Even if several months or years will elapse before you'll be applying for a job, now is the time to prepare. If you haven't already started, begin learning *now* how you can go about finding job opportunities in the career you're pursuing. Put together a resume *today*—before you find yourself forced to develop one at the last minute. Collect all of the information you're likely to need to complete a job application and keep it organized in a file, updating it regularly. Attend job interview workshops whenever they're offered, and seek one-on-one assistance from a career counselor if you think it will help. The key is to be prepared for what lies ahead. Exactly how prepared you're going to be when the time comes to obtain a job is up to only one person . . . and that person is *you!*

Summary of Important Tips for Job Interview Preparation

- Attend job interview workshops.
- Practice interview skills with a family member or friend.
- Dress professionally (no matter what type of job it is).
- Examine and clean up your online profile.
- Find out about the company through research.
- Anticipate the questions you'll be asked and prepare answers accordingly.
- Be prepared to ask questions of the interviewer.
- Find out how to get to the interview location well in advance.

Appendix E

By completing a job satisfaction questionnaire, you'll be able to identify those aspects of your current job that are rewarding as well as those that contribute to dissatisfaction. The results will help you clarify the aspects of a job that most directly contribute to your career satisfaction. You can also use this exercise to predict how you *might* respond to *potential* occupations and the degree of satisfaction that a potential job is likely to provide.

PART I

General Information

Occupation: _____

How long have you worked for this company? _____

What previous positions have you held with the company?

_____

_____

What is your job title? _____

How long have you held your current position? _____

Briefly describe your work responsibilities (as you would on a resume):

_____

_____

_____

_____

_____

PART II
RATING YOUR CURRENT JOB SATISFACTION

1	2	3	4	5
not satisfied at all		*somewhat satisfied*		*extremely satisfied*

Using the scale shown above, rate your level of satisfaction with the following aspects of your job.

General Working Conditions

_____ Hours worked each week

_____ Flexibility in scheduling

_____ Location of work

_____ Amount of paid vacation time/sick leave offered

Pay and Promotion Potential

_____ Salary

_____ Opportunities for promotion

_____ Benefits (health insurance, life insurance, etc.)

_____ Job security

_____ Recognition for work accomplished

Work Relationships

_____ Relationships with your coworkers

_____ Relationship(s) with your supervisor(s)

_____ Relationships with your subordinates (if applicable)

Use of Skills and Abilities

_____ Opportunity to use your skills and talents

_____ Opportunity to learn new skills

_____ Support for additional training and education

Work Activities

_____ Variety of job responsibilities

_____ Degree of independence associated with your work roles

_____ Adequate opportunity for periodic changes in duties

Other Aspects of the Job Relating to Your Level of Satisfaction

_____

_____

_____

_____

_____

Review your ratings. List the items below for which your satisfaction level is a 4 or a 5:

_____

_____

_____

_____

_____

_____

These are the generally satisfying aspects of your current job. As you consider potential career changes, take into account those things about your current job that are particularly satisfying.

Now list the items below for which your satisfaction level is a 1 or a 2.

_____

_____

_____

_____

_____

_____

These are the dissatisfying characteristics associated with your current job. They are the types of things that you'll want to avoid in any future career or occupational choice. You can gain a better understanding of what to look for in a future career by analyzing what you dislike about your current job.

Bibliography

Dikel, M. R., & Roehm, F. E. (2002). *Guide to Internet job searching.* New York: McGraw Hill.

Farr, J. M., & Shatkin, L. (2004). *The O*NET dictionary of occupational titles* (3rd ed.). Indianapolis: JIST Works.

Ferguson Publishing. (2007). *Encyclopedia of careers and vocational guidance* (14th ed.). Chicago: Author.

Gottfredson, G. D., & Holland, J. L. (1996). *Dictionary of Holland occupational codes* (3rd ed.). Lutz, FL: Psychological Assessment Resources.

Hammer, A. L. (1993). *Introduction to type and careers.* Palo Alto, CA: Consulting Psychologists Press.

Harris-Bowlsbey, J., Dikel, M. R., & Sampson, J. P., Jr. (2002). *The Internet: A tool for career planning* (2nd ed.). Broken Arrow, OK: National Career Development Association.

Mitchell, K. (2003). *The unplanned career: How to turn curiosity into opportunity.* San Francisco: Chronicle Books.

Niles, S. G., Goodman, J., & Pope, M. (2002). *The career counseling casebook: A resource for practitioners, students, and counselor educators.* Broken Arrow, OK: National Career Development Association.

Occupational information network. (http://online.onetcenter.org). Washington, DC: U.S. Department of Labor.

Occupational outlook handbook. (http://www.bls.gov/oco/). Washington, DC: U.S. Department of Labor.

Shahnasarian, M. (2006). *Decision time: A guide to career enhancement* (3rd ed.). Broken Arrow, OK: National Career Development Association.

Taylor, J., & Hardy, D. (2004). *Monster careers: How to land the job of your life.* New York: Penguin Books.

Tieger, P. D., & Barron-Tieger, B. (2007). *Do what you are: Discover the perfect career for you through the secrets of personality type* (4th ed.). New York: Little, Brown and Company.

Wall, J. E. (2005). *What do I like to do? 101 activities to identify interests and plan careers.* Austin, TX: Pro-Ed.

Index